A Brief History of the Future

A Brief History of the Future

The United States in a Changing World Order

Allan E. Goodman

WESTVIEW PRESS

Boulder • San Francisco • Oxford

Copyright © 1993 by Westview Press, Inc.

Published in 1993 in the United States of America by Westview Press, Inc., 5500 Central Avenue, Boulder, Colorado 80301-2877, and in the United Kingdom by Westview Press, 36 Lonsdale Road, Summertown, Oxford OX2 7EW

Library of Congress Cataloging-in-Publication Data
Goodman, Allan E., 1944–
   A brief history of the future: the United States in a changing world order / by Allan E. Goodman.
      p.   cm.
   Includes bibliographical references and index.
   ISBN 0-8133-1620-0.   ISBN 0-8133-1621-9 (pbk.)
   1. United States—Foreign relations—1989–   2. World politics—1989–   I. Title.
E840.G66   1993
327'.09'049—dc20   92-41983
                                                              CIP

Printed and bound in the United States of America

The paper used in this publication meets the requirements
of the American National Standard for Permanence of Paper
for Printed Library Materials Z39.48-1984.

10   9   8   7   6   5   4   3   2   1

For Danielle, George, and Allan John

Contents

Tables

Acknowledgments

Five hundred years after Christopher Columbus persuaded the Spanish monarchy to underwrite exploration his contemporaries had ridiculed, museum visitors in Washington had a chance to see why discovery beckoned. Called *Circa 1492*, some 569 artifacts of all types from around the time that Columbus sailed for what he thought would be China but turned out to be a new world were gathered at the National Gallery of Art. The exhibit provided a look at how rich the imagination of humankind was even at the beginning of the Renaissance.

The exhibition showed the state of our global thinking at the time Columbus set off. I was startled to see how quickly we left the Dark Ages behind us and were able to make a transition from thinking about the world of the village and the cloister to the world beyond the cities and microstates in which we lived. I marveled at how far the desire for trade and its benefits took essentially ordinary people as well as egotists like Columbus. With such trade, I saw, not only was everyday life enriched, but our aspirations and reach were enlarged. And I was deeply struck by the central role vision appeared to play in making it possible for Columbus and the discoverers in every culture at the time to have their dreams about what lay ahead and where.

At the beginning of the exhibition was a beautiful map drawn in 1375 at Majorca by a skilled draftsman who had to be part cartographer and part visionary. Scholars of the period think this person was named Abraham Cresques; I think he must have been extraordinary. The map, known today as the *Catalan Atlas*, contains much that is wrong and includes sketches from portions of a world that Cresques could not have actually known to exist. But he aimed at making a representation based on everything: secret and other closely held charts of the navigators of the era, books by and reports from travelers to the farthest-flung parts of the known earth, and the predominant myths, legends, and religious teachings then used to explain known and surmised geographical facts. Places Cresques could not have visited or from which he could not have had reliable reports from those who did, he imagined. And in so doing, his atlas showed people like Columbus and the rulers on whom they came to depend that the world could be far greater and more interesting than the immediate surroundings of their court. Cresques also appended to his maps a set of theories about how the earth itself was related to the cosmos and about the dynamics of the forces thought to determine those fundamental elements that affected daily life no matter where one lived.

This book is also an attempt to provide a representation of a world in which none of us have lived and of its potential dynamics. My "sources" are as varied as those Abraham Cresques used to develop his atlas, and the results may be as flawed. But the whole point was to try to envision a world fundamentally different and better than we have known during the cold war era.

The idea to undertake such a forecast and write such a book took shape in my mind while preparing an address I was asked to give at the 92nd commencement exercises of Mount Ida College. I thank that college's president, Dr. Brian Carlson, and the trustees for inviting me to do so; Dr. Carlson is himself deeply engaged in thinking about new futures for U.S. colleges and my work on this book also benefited from reflecting on the strategy and position papers he prepared in launching the college's Naples Institute. I am also very grateful for the encouragement and superb support given by Jennifer Knerr and her editorial colleagues Libby Barstow and Cheryl Carnahan at Westview Press. Nothing is more helpful to an author than a publisher like Westview that is enthusiastic and also critical at just the right times and spaces.

While writing, I was fortunate to have the chance to share my forecast with participants in the Georgetown Leadership Seminar and the IBM International Personnel Institutes held at the School of Foreign Service in 1991 and 1992. My research assistant, Sandra C. McMahon, with whom I have also written another Westview book entitled *Making Peace*, did much to help me fill in the blanks and detect the discontinuities that developed as I wrote; she also compiled the Appendix and contributed the special focus and "dateline" features that occur in most chapters. Susan Lubick supplied important but hard-to-find data about world technological developments and U.S. government operations. The following colleagues read and critiqued the manuscript at various stages: Madeleine Albright, Hans Binnendijk, Maria Carland, Chester Crocker, Harm De Blij, Peter Dunkley, Theodore Geiger, David Gries, Gary Hufbauer, Peter F. Krogh, Louis Marmon, M.D., John McNeil, Theodore Moran, David Newsom, Henry Nowik, H. K. Ranftle, Richard Scribner, David Taylor, Seth Tillman, and Abiodun Williams. The students who took my spring 1992 seminar on analysis and forecasting provided constant reference points for and tenacious arguments with what I was planning to write. Andrew D'Uva, Executive Assistant at the School of Foreign Service, helped greatly in acquiring and applying the latest technology to convert a manuscript of many parts into a text ready for printing.

To all: Thank you.

Allan E. Goodman

1

Introduction

The future is happening faster than any of us can imagine. I learned just how fast in October 1989 when I gave a lecture to a group of young scholars from West Germany and predicted that the Berlin Wall would be torn down and their country reunited sometime before the end of the century. Not a single person in the room agreed with me, and many considered it a highly unlikely prospect even within their lifetimes. Less than a month later, we were both proved wrong: The Wall came down, and much sooner than even I had anticipated.

But my message to the group was that our world would be increasingly shaped by swift and largely unexpected changes that would challenge our existing theories and our views of what might be possible for the future. Ahead, I forecast, lay a period of considerable upheaval—conceptual as well as political. As a result, I also suggested that by the year 2000, there would be at least 200 members of the United Nations versus the 161 that were in the General Assembly in 1989. Within eighteen months of my making that forecast, nearly twenty new nations were in the process of being created as a result of the breakup of the Soviet Union and the fracturing of certain nations in Eastern Europe.

The continuation of the processes of such change and upheaval will have profound and largely unforeseeable consequences for the nature of international affairs. New structures and relationships will be only partly conceived from those of the past international system. New rules and fresh actors will appear in response to the needs of the future system, and old theories and assumptions will become obsolete as a result of the altered global scene. Anticipating the new directions of the future and comprehending the forces and dynamics that are transforming the map of our world—and the U.S. role in this changing world order—are the topics of this book. As such, I have written it both for specialists, who may be interested in designing American foreign policy and projecting the U.S. global and regional roles in the future, as well as for general readers who are trying to make sense out of what is going on. The scope and reach of the book cover some very broad ground because the future will undoubtedly widen our horizons and require a deep and thoughtful American engagement in world events.

There is, of course, no bona fide branch of science that enables us to predict the future accurately. Crystal balls, tarot cards, and Ouija boards may be just as effective as the so-called scientific formulas developed in the 1970s and 1980s by world power assessors and political risk analysis firms for making forecasts and predictions. And even today, some political leaders would not think of developing policies about the future without first consulting their astrologers. In any case, analyses that look ahead need to offer commonsense assumptions about the impact of the past as well as an assessment of the degree to which a linear projection of the future is likely to prove inadequate. Consequently, such work requires an ability to envision what might happen, to deduce why a particular sequence of events is most plausible, and to imagine the consequences and aftermath of such events.

In this book, I argue that the future is far brighter than any Americans have studied or contemplated since the end of World War II. This optimistic prediction, in itself, is a difficult prospect for many to accept. Just a few years ago, Barbara Tuchman's book *A Distant Mirror*, which dealt with life (but mostly death) in the fourteenth century, offered a sober glimpse of what most thought would lie ahead. Few of us had much trouble, when the book appeared, accepting the striking parallels between the darkest part of the Middle Ages and the outlook for the international system in the 1970s and 1980s. Like our distant forebears, we were (and still are) facing a plague of global proportions. The human immunodeficiency virus (HIV) has the potential to wipe out entire races and possibly some countries. The end of the cold war and with it the end of the nuclear arms race seemed remote possibilities at the time of Tuchman's book, and the probability that such ends were in sight continued to decline sharply for most of the 1980s. Wars and terrorism resulting from religious fanaticism seemed likely to spread from the Middle East to much of the industrialized world. And to many, a cataclysmic struggle between elemental forces loomed ahead, the outcome of which had the potential to make the living envy the dead. Many prophets pessimistically predicted that Armageddon was closer at hand than the Third Millennium if the conflict somehow escalated to nuclear war.

Clearly, our expectations have altered, and so should our optic. The degree of change in the world is so overwhelming and so promising, in fact, that I now think the past—and especially the patterns of thinking and acting during the cold war era—actually limits our ability to imagine the future.

A few years ago, in fact, historians and political scientists alike were engaged in a debate over whether the end of the cold war and the apparent victory of liberal democracy over all ideological contenders—particularly communism—signaled the end of history. Dr. Francis Fukuyama of the RAND Corporation theorized that world history could be viewed as a dialectical evolutionary process, and he further hypothesized that the victory of economic and political liberalism marked the culmination of man's rational ideological evolution. An argument ensued over the degree to which the dynamics of domestic and world politics would continue to be shaped by familiar ideas and concepts. Based on the Fukuyama theory, what's ahead would be a direct extension of the ideas and actions that won—ended is probably a better term to describe the events of 1989-1990—the cold war. In this case, although the future would not necessarily be surprise- or trouble-free, the challenges it would pose could eventually be surmounted by a more perfect implementation of democratic values and systems.

Dr. Fukuyama was serving as a member of the State Department's Policy Planning Council at the time his article appeared. Since his views were assumed to be representative of at least some segment of the U.S. foreign policy decisionmaking establishment, interest in his prediction that we were unlikely to witness the emergence of any new ideas that would define power and alignments in international affairs was heightened. Dr. Fukuyama has since published an important book, *The End of History and the Last Man*, expounding on his theory, but his period of service in the government has ended. As I suggest later, we are probably the poorer for it, because Dr. Fukuyama has imagination and vision, qualities that are essential to creating the policies and the institutions the United States will need to cope with what's ahead.

I do not accept all of Fukuyama's arguments, however. To me, the history of the international system is composed of ideas and their impact on human behavior as well as the unexpected occurrences and coincidences, at both the macro and micro levels, that shape world politics by affecting national and individual responses. Accordingly, in this book I focus especially on the role of certain ideas, inventions, and trends that are shaping the present and will determine the future. The history of the future, then, is the projection of how such forces and dynamics could affect the conditions of world politics tomorrow. Just as it is possible for the professional historian to infer from incomplete records why people acted the way they did in the past, I think it is possible to infer how they will act in the future, as long as we are clear about the ideas that give rise to such action. Hence, this particular "history" begins by trying to identify the ideas that are changing the map of the modern world and how they will surprise us in shaping the international system from now until well into the twenty-first century.

Another reason I am writing this book is because of my conviction that we have greeted the end of the cold war with altogether too much pessimism and self-doubt. Because we were surprised by the way in which our conflict with the Soviet Union ended—and especially at the way in which the Soviet state and Communist party disintegrated—we had no well-thought-out response, and how we did respond was accompanied by a great deal of suspicion over who in Moscow was in charge of relations with the United States and what their motives might be. Consequently, we did not readily embrace the changes we had hoped for, and spent precious months debating over whether and then how we should aid Russian leaders in their transition away from communism. The results were paltry in comparison with what was needed to avoid despair and trouble in the countries of the former Soviet Union. This should not have been the case.

I found such responses occurred because essentially we lacked a vision of what was ahead and what we wanted the new world order to be—for us as well as for others. In one sense we wanted the world to be free without having to help it to become so. The U.S. reluctance to engage in yet another great crusade was understandable. We had bankrupted ourselves in fighting the cold war as well as several others, and we did not have the resources needed to tackle problems simultaneously at home and abroad.

By the time this book appears, the immediate crises of the post-cold war period will somehow have been surmounted. But this will not have lessened the need for a long-term vision and a plan to achieve that vision. Moreover, precisely because we lacked a policy for creating the new world order from the outset, we run a real risk of failing to develop one once immediate crises have passed by, thinking that the future will take care of itself. Such order will not be created over the course of a few eventful and tumultuous years. And the United States has a very big stake in the direction the international system will take as well as in the way in which the conflicts of this period will be resolved. Anyone, of course, can say there will be conflicts ahead that we cannot avoid or do much to prevent. But this is no reason to forgo thinking about a world in which our goals can be achieved and then about the design of the courses of action we might want to follow to achieve those goals. And because the road to attaining our objectives is likely to be expensive (though less so by a considerable margin than during the cold war), we need a plan around which a consensus can be built.

So one way to get the process started is to think not only about what might lie ahead but about what we would like the future to contain. And it is in this spirit that I have written the present book. It is easy to envision what could go wrong with the scenarios to be discussed here and why the chances of achieving this kind of future might seem to be rather slim. But such thinking does us little good because it does not detail the actions we could be taking to promote U.S. interests in a changing world order that actually brings us a century of peace and global economic development. Thus, there is a need for bold imaginings as well as leadership to create the conditions under which we give ourselves the greatest chance of success in realizing a world order without war and one that has as its core purpose the extension of human progress and freedom.

The method of the study is to imagine the future as being shaped largely by the interaction of four central forces—democratization, technological innovation, regional integration, and the obsolescence of war—and their impact on economic and political behavior. The rise and consequences of these forces have already changed what we think is possible for politics. Five years ago we were extremely pessimistic about the prospects for democracy in the Third World, let alone in Eastern Europe or the Soviet Union; we were still reluctant to export many technologies because of the way they could be used to tighten the grip of dictatorial regimes; European integration was seen as leading only to "Eurosclerosis"; and, when 1986 was declared the U.N. Year of Peace, more wars were being fought than at any time since the end of World War II and the international organization itself was widely thought to be moribund. The forces mentioned above, however, have already demonstrated their power to change the nature of world politics and the dynamics of the international system. The challenge now is to assess how they might continue to do so and how we will want the changes they are bringing to affect our global future.

2

The Forecast

The twenty-first century will encompass the longest period of peace, democracy, and economic development in history. The new century will be an intercultural one. The great and transcendent forces of the age—the idea of freedom and the application of technology to make people everywhere both freer and more able to control their environment—will erode national boundaries and, eventually, the concept of sovereignty itself will become obsolete. Even though the landmarks of the twenty-first century may contain such structures as former Soviet president Gorbachev's "common European house," a Pacific Basin Commonwealth, and the North American Common Market, the politics of the century will not be shaped by a *Pax Americana* or the ideology of any other single power. Thus, a new world order will be created but without the trauma and conflict associated with past attempts by hegemonic powers to dictate an international balance of power.

For all practical purposes, the twenty-first century began in 1989, heralded by the fall of the Berlin Wall. And by the end of Operation Desert Storm, the nature of world politics had been substantially—but not completely—transformed. As is already evident in the aftermath of the Gulf war, the degree to which military power influences people and events is steadily declining. And as is clear in such diverse places as Russia, South Korea, and South Africa, the influence of democratic ideals and "people power" is far more potent and much more unpredictable than any strategist of the 1980s would have forecast.

Although we have yet to comprehend fully the dynamics behind and thrust of such sources of political power and change, we already know they are quite different from the great power politics we have been so used to seeing and analyzing in international affairs. For nearly the entire twentieth century, the way great powers acted and what they wanted (for good as well as for ill) were in large part foreseeable. Nations operated according to declared grand strategies and with a great degree of consistency as part of alliances with great powers. The advent of people power is already changing all this. Rather than grand strategies, what is emerging in countries undergoing the transformation from communism and other forms of dictatorship to free market and political systems is a persistent and tumultuous quest for internal security, ethnic self-determination, and improvement in the material quality of life. As populations become freer—and I think this is the inevitable, albeit longer-term result of the political and societal changes we are now seeing—the nature of and threats to the international system will also be much less determined by reference to great-power politics. Even though great disparities in national objectives and relative wealth will still exist among states, world politics will become less focused on the needs of the wealthy and be far less responsive to the ambitions of the militarily powerful.

The central diplomatic questions of our time, are what system will replace the outmoded one, which has unraveled, and what principles will frame the new organization? In a certain eerie sense, we are again at a time so prophetically described by Bismarck when he likened the European powers of his era—and their desire for balance and stability among them—to strangers traveling on a train who are nervous in each other's presence. The fear, of course, arises from the premise that as one of the travelers begins to move, the others will feel compelled to react defensively before they have determined everyone's intentions. Consequently, the security of each can only be achieved at the insecurity of the others.

Fortunately, several trends make me think we will now survive the current period without generating the types of mutual suspicions and reactions that led to initiating a drive toward a military buildup at the end of the last century and to war in the early part of the present one. They are:

- the increasing movement toward democratization in the greater and lesser powers of the international system and the clear recognition of the deep and enduring interdependence among them;
- the impact of possessing considerably greater knowledge of and ability to communicate about the actions that enhance or threaten security and prosperity;
- the declining utility and affordability of force as an instrument of foreign policy; and
- the development of a robust system of global and regional organization on which to build a new world order.

Now over time, functions of such international organizations will probably become much more specialized in an effort to achieve a greater degree of coherence and operational effectiveness. And as both of these objectives are realized—sometime toward the end of the first half of the twenty-first century—international organizations will increasingly acquire the attributes of regional collective security systems, with the term "security" defined in the broadest possible terms to include everything from basic human needs to human rights. By mid-century, in fact, state sovereignty will have eroded to the point where it will be possible to conclude that the age of nations has truly passed.

The fact that the nation-state as we think of it will no longer be the principal unit for conducting "international" relationships does not mean that legally recognized organizations to provide domestic welfare beyond the family, corporation, or village will be unnecessary. The provision and maintenance of safe water and secure food supplies, the protection against those forces that will tend to threaten or violate established orders, and the regulation of activities designed to care for, house, and transport people will all require some form of sociopolitical organization. But what will be different about the world of the next century is the extent to which we discover that many such domestic functions of government can be served by a variety of authorities and at a range of levels, as well as the fact that it may be within our interests and capabilities to have such diversity and complexity. To serve domestic welfare functions, consequently, some organizations may need to be much larger than any with which Americans are presently familiar. For example, instead of having each of many separate states on the eastern seaboard of the United States regulate road and rail networks and electrical and water supplies, we may find it both practicable and desirable to have a single "mega-authority" do the same job. The European Community is already doing this in literally hundreds of areas despite once formidable cultural and linguistic barriers, and many Americans living in rural areas have now had nearly a half century of experience in looking to vast regional cooperatives to provide water, flood control, and electricity.

The point is that in the future, the technology for government to communicate and act at all levels and of the great public utilities to provide services is going to make it possible for people to fulfill their needs in the most cost-effective manner rather than as a local function of the jurisdiction in which they happen to reside. As this occurs, we are likely to invent new forms and units of governance, which may not parallel the geographical and legal boundaries or even the form of the state system of the twentieth century.

The Forces Shaping the Future

The most important paradigm for understanding the future organization and evolution of the international system along these lines will be democratically-induced societal change. This concept refers to the interaction among the expansion of political participation, the emergence of free market economic systems, and the secularization of culture. When these developments occur simultaneously, people and governments are empowered to define new goals and ways of achieving them. This type of societal change is particularly significant in turn because it substantially raises expectations for freedom, makes the political culture less exclusive, and dramatically increases demands for widespread economic development and human rights, which eventually generate transformations of governmental systems. Such transformations are already under way on the entire European, South American, and South Asian continents, as well as in rapidly industrializing developing countries of North and Southeast Asia, southern Africa, and the Middle East.

Although it is used occasionally by the U.S. intelligence community to develop long-range political forecasts, the paradigm is not widely applied in either the academic or popular literature as an approach to understanding contemporary problems in the field of international relations (IR). For most professional as well as amateur IR theorists (ranging from Joseph Nye at Harvard, to Paul Kennedy at Yale, to Alvin Toffler of *Powershift* fame), the central tools for the study of power—and how it is created, used, transferred, balanced, and diffused—are the gauges that measure the amounts of and relationship among national wealth, military might, and the structure of the international system. I think, however, that observation of the forces and dynamics of societal change will prove to be a more effective means of gauging the aspirations that shape and challenge the international order in the twenty-first century than the traditional indicators used to measure national power in the twentieth century. Moreover, this paradigm will help to explain a phenomenon that will be central to the conduct of foreign policy in the period immediately ahead—namely, why the application of large amounts of force and other forms of national power may still fail to produce influence and control in international affairs.

How did we get to this point?

What Happened

When the Berlin Wall was permanently breached on 9 November 1989, newspapers printed inaccurate headlines. What should have been proclaimed was the following:

WORLD WAR II OVER. GERMANY AND JAPAN VICTORIOUS.
U.S. AND RUSSIA BROKE.

The events of 1989-1990 symbolized not only the end of the cold war but also the end of the forty-year campaign to integrate the German and Japanese economies and nationalistic drives into the international system. This restructuring has demanded that the United States and the leaders of the former Soviet Union sanction the incorporation of both countries into regional and international positions of power, at enormous long-term costs to the former superpowers. In order for Berlin—and the rest of Eastern Europe—to be liberated, the Soviet Union's leadership was forced to concede that a powerful Germany no longer posed a security threat; some time earlier, the United States and its allies in Asia were compelled to reach a similar conclusion regarding Japan.

In order for both Germany and Japan to contain their nationalistic aspirations and the inherent tendency to dominate their respective regions, a substitute for the accumulation of prestige through military power and a diversion for the vast energy and wealth of these countries had to be discovered. Ironically, unhampered economic growth and unfettered access to world trade proved to be the remedies. This outcome is ironic because, at least in the case of Japan, it ultimately secured the goals of the autocrats who had led the country into World War II. Therefore, some Japanese have currently boasted that despite their country's World War II military defeat, they have now managed to achieve many of their original nationalistic and economic objectives.

Japan probably has a far greater global role to play and distance to go in adapting to a changed world order than Germany, and the Japanese have much more difficulty in coming to terms with such a destiny, especially when pressed to do so by the United States. A half century ago, U.S. and Japanese leaders were oblivious to the needs of one another and eventually took actions that incited the two nations to go to war without necessarily wanting to do so. What we knew of Japan at the time came from a series of books, impressions, and memoirs—the majority of which were written by people with virtually no access to the inner circle of leaders shaping Japan's politics and foreign relations. Some of this "knowledge" was derived, moreover, from the experience of those missionaries who had tried to bring Christianity to the Far East; their actions involved suppressing rather than comprehending the nature of Japanese culture and popular spirit. The picture, surprisingly, is not much different today. Is it our destiny to misunderstand and alienate each other?

Reading the newspapers over the past few years, one would certainly think so. Hardly a week goes by without one or another U.S. or Japanese politician making an offending statement. On the American side, we cannot seem to penetrate the barriers to competition in Japan's markets, and we surmise that there is a conscious effort afoot to exclude us and our goods from those markets. Although few U.S. homes exist without a myriad of products we gladly purchase from the Japanese, we chafe at the stories we have heard about the neighbor or business associate who has been the victim of Japan's customs procedures, which prevent many U.S. goods and services from entering Japan. The reality that more Americans today probably owe their jobs to Japanese than to American automakers has not translated into even the most modest increase in respect for Japanese people or culture in our country. In fact, when

Japanese come calling with large amounts of cash to acquire real estate, many local communities react with vocal complaints and express profound unease at accepting foreign owners and neighbors, no matter how depressed the current market.

Recent international events and crises, moreover, have done nothing to improve the situation. Even though the Japanese government contributed about $13 billion to the success of Operation Desert Storm, it did so only reluctantly and in a way that invited little thanks. The Japanese people—who work at least as hard as Americans and who pay new taxes with the same degree of reluctance—had a difficult time understanding what they would receive for their monetary investment, and the way in which the money was extracted did little to reassure the citizens or to help their political leaders make the case that Japan would gain greater international respect by contributing. Although Japan participates in the economic summit among U.S., Canadian, British, French, German, and Italian leaders that takes place annually, its leaders seem to remain perpetually in the dark about international affairs and the initiatives that would lend themselves to multilateral action.

The U.S.-Japanese relationship is continuing to deteriorate, moreover, despite a series of encounters and exchanges of information at all levels that may be the most intense and interconnected of those between any two countries at any time in history. Such a knowledge flow should not have led to the misunderstanding and tension that exist today. Japanese visitors represent the group that contributes the most to the U.S. tourist industry on an annual basis. Each day, millions of words are faxed back and forth between America and Japan. Total investment in each country by individuals and firms owned or headquartered in the other is measured in the tens of billions, the largest such overseas investment between any two countries. Finally, a large portion of the U.S. public debt in T-bills is owned by Japanese investors.

Japan today reflects a surprisingly large number of U.S. values. The Japanese constitution was written by an American military commander. At the end of World War II, the defeat of Japan was accompanied by an unconditional surrender as well as instructions to the Japanese people from their emperor to obey the Americans. As a result, in no other society has U.S. influence been so fully extended or felt, our values and institutions so clearly legislated, or our ways and technological innovations so faithfully applied.

In contrast, Americans receive very little news about Japan. During an average week, the *New York Times*, the *Wall Street Journal*, and the *Washington Post* may carry hardly any stories on topics related to Japan. In local papers in major cities, the number is probably no more than one story every month. Often these stories contain fewer than 100 words, and about half of the press coverage of Japan may be limited to a photograph with a caption. For example, during the week I began to formulate this forecast, there was only one "story" about Japan in any of the three newspapers mentioned above. It consisted of a photograph of Diet members in a melee as a result of a committee meeting where the chairman attempted to push through a vote. This picture may remain in the minds of countless numbers of readers of these three newspapers for the next six months as the only illustration of the functioning of Japan's parliamentary system. In the Japanese papers news about the United States appears daily.

Today, many pairs of countries have extensive economic and commercial interactions, but the flow of genuine knowledge about each other is much smaller. However, despite this expanded sharing of knowledge, my sense of things is that the degree of mutual misunderstanding between Japan and the United States is virtually unique. Unfortunately, it does not appear to be improving significantly.

Yet I can think of no other two countries in which such a large variety of cultural as well as scholarly and political institutions spend more money on communications and dialogue. Each encounter, however, has resulted in relatively little benefit. Such meetings involve specialists, who either have a particular ax to grind or who already know their counterparts quite well. Each meeting begins and ends with the litany that the U.S.-Japan relationship is the most important that either country maintains. In truth, the Americans don't really believe this, and the Japanese—having heard it so often and from such a wide variety of top government officials, educators, and business people—don't doubt it. The result is shock on the Japanese part when our actions serve to alienate them, and a certain degree of forgetfulness on the U.S. part when we prepare to undertake major projects in international affairs without giving much thought to how and when we should consult with the Japanese government.

Consequently, Japanese intellectuals and political leaders today manifest a degree of dislike for the United States that is unprecedented in half a century. The Gulf crisis, moreover, worsened the relationship, leaving many Japanese to conclude that Americans think of their country, according to a recent article in *Foreign Affairs* by the diplomatic correspondent of the *Asahi Shimbun*, as "an automatic teller machine—one that needed a kick before dispensing the cash." And there have been abundant signs over the past several years that the Japanese are readying to kick back economically by continuing to resist the elimination of their notorious nontariff barriers to U.S. products and by becoming more outspoken in criticism of the way we manage our economy and culture. The problem with the U.S.-Japanese relationship is that at the strategic level, it has not kept pace with the changes taking place in international affairs, and the leaders have not been able to develop a formula for genuine consultations about how they can work in tandem to shape the future. Instead, the relationship at the top is bogged down over technical trade issues that, although important to resolve, do not promote discussion of how the two countries can and should respond to the broad array of post-cold war era challenges.

In the case of Germany, part of the incentive for initiating a regional war was the issue of national boundaries—geographic and economic—and the extent to which its neighbors could be effectively controlled and gradually overwhelmed. Obviously, Germany has not obtained the European territorial empire to which Hitler and his generals aspired in the late 1930s. However, today Germany commands the status of the largest and single most important country in Europe. The economic futures of its eastern neighbors are as dependent upon their integration into a Greater Deutschmark Zone as on their access to an expanded European Community. Germany also wanted to control, if not disarm, Russia. Both of these long-forgotten objectives could be realized by the end of the 1990s.

What the leaders of the superpowers in the 1980s and early 1990s did not anticipate, of course, was the speed with which the trend toward democratization would unfold, accompanying the failure of socialism in Asia and Stalinism in central Europe. They also failed to predict the impoverished state of their own national economies at that time. Consequently, neither Soviet nor U.S. policy could retard or accelerate the process of democratic conversion in its initial stages.

Here it might be useful to examine an international affairs chronology for the 1980s, such as the one contained in the Appendix to this book. From Poland to the Philippines and back again to Poland, from China to Czechoslovakia, from South Africa to South Korea to the Soviet Union, the focus of events throughout the entire decade of the 1980s centered on dialogue and experimentation regarding the most potent force in human history: the idea of freedom.

Thus, the forces behind the transformation of the international system and the relative power of the United States within that system reveal very deep roots. This is a point that is seldom presented in a discussion of the dramatic episodes of 1989-1990. In fact, these events are now routinely characterized as "revolutionary." We did not witness a classic revolution in the sense of a rapid but also violent and fundamental break with the core values and procedures that underlie the international system. Although the numbers and capabilities of key players in the system may have altered, many of these modifications in international relationships and domestic political systems were conceptually quite familiar. The novelty was the speed with which they occurred and the unique interactions and repercussions felt among events in various locations.

Although it is certainly correct to single out Soviet president Gorbachev as the most significant catalyst to new conditions in world politics, it is important to recall that many of the ideas on which the international system is being built today were those entertained by his predecessors and developed by other pioneers in the 1970s and even the 1960s. For example, the appeal of the late

Alexander Dubcek's "Prague Spring" experiment illustrated the widespread endorsement of the ideas of individual freedom and economic development in Eastern Europe. In a similar sense, the extensive past debate over the late Willy Brandt's ideas for *ost politik* probably made possible the rapid development of consensus in Germany and much of Europe over the issue of reunification. U.S. leaders have also made substantial contributions to the concepts, and the momentum behind them that are currently shaping the international environment. President Richard Nixon and Henry Kissinger developed an essentially new theory of détente in Soviet-U.S. relations in the early 1970s and proved that cooperation was feasible on a step-by-step, issue-by-issue basis. In the scheme of this strategy, areas of controversy such as Vietnam, Panama, or even Lithuania were not necessarily viewed as impediments to arms control or other agreements. This novel approach paved the way for scientific and technical cooperation on a broad range of issues during the cold war era and now in the present one. When President Jimmy Carter established human rights as a central U.S. foreign policy objective in the mid-1970s, this decision not only elevated the importance attached to the Helsinki process in Europe but also encouraged democratization efforts elsewhere around the globe.

Therefore, the current changes in our international system are grounded in deep historical roots and are propelled by an increasing momentum. For the most part, these transformations have not been revolutionary, in classical political terms. Although the ideas precipitating such change can be categorized as fundamental breaks with orthodoxy, they are also quite familiar. In many of the most significant cases, the changes were not preceded by violent upheaval—although in some cases violence has been the result (e.g., the coup attempts in the wake of prodemocratic regime changes in Haiti and the Philippines, the crackdown on the prodemocracy demonstration in Tiananmen Square in China, and the Russian military assaults on secession movements in the Baltics). Presumably, then, a considerable amount of change—and conflict generated by its speed and scope—still lies ahead.

What's Ahead?

Democracy will not work everywhere initially, nor will free trade and global interdependence benefit all immediately. Expectations are being created that cannot be fulfilled. And no matter how well-intentioned, a number of current leaders will fail to overcome systemic and structural obstacles to change, whereas others will be removed from power because they were viewed as perpetuating the old order in their quest for social stability. In some countries, consequently, governments will change rapidly and unpredictably. On the economic front, the period ahead in world politics will reveal that many states do not possess effective control over their currencies, whereas others will lack the ability to control entire sectors of their economies. Even today, no state possesses the power actually required to protect its environment, and very few, if any, have the resources and reach to provide security unilaterally. In short, the downfall of dictators does not assure that those behind the movement toward democratization will have the necessary experience to govern wisely or well or that rapid political change will automatically produce the consensus among citizens to undertake the extraordinary work required to make the world better than they found it. It will be crucial for effective foreign policy management, therefore, to anticipate the distinctive mix of economic conditions, cultural reactions, and political upheaval that could potentially lead to stress and conflict over the changes ahead at the societal as well as the political level. Consider, for example, the headlines "reproduced" below, which may actually appear over the next several years.

1993-1994

U.S./CANADA/MEXICO FREE TRADE AGREEMENT SIGNED
MEXICAN LEADERS AGREE TO FORM COALITION
EARTHQUAKES ROCK CALIFORNIA TO CENTRAL AMERICA
CIVIL WAR ERUPTS IN PANAMA

GORBACHEV NAMED TO TOP U.N. POST

UK WITHDRAWS FORCES FROM NORTHERN IRELAND
CSCE CREATES STANDING MILITARY COMMISSION
KOHL PARTY SUFFERS MAJOR DEFEAT
WALESA GOVERNMENT FALLS
UKRAINE BREAD RIOTS

ARAFAT ASSASSINATED
SAUDI MONARCH OVERTHROWN
PLO DISBANDED

U.S. RECOGNIZES VIETNAM
PRC RECALLS ALL STUDENTS FROM ABROAD
CAMBODIAN PEACE ARRANGEMENTS FAIL; 3D WAR BEGINS
SUHARTO PREVENTED FROM SEEKING NEW TERM
CHINA LEADERS CALL FOR CULTURAL PURIFICATION

INDIA USES NUCLEAR WEAPON IN KASHMIR WAR

SECOND INDIAN STATE SECEDES

WORLD FOOD BANK ESTABLISHED FOR AFRICA
MOST POOR NATIONS' DEBT CANCELLED IN NATURE SWAP

SHINING PATH AND DRUG LORDS OVERTHROW FUJIMORI

QUEBEC SECEDES
SAVANNAH RIVER NUCLEAR PLANT DEVASTATED
U.S. AND FRANCE FORM RAPID DEPLOYMENT FORCE

KNESSET APPROVES SELF-GOVERNMENT FOR WEST BANK
IRAN MODERATES OVERTHROW ISLAMIC GOVERNMENT
JORDAN CONFEDERATES WITH WEST BANK
MUBARAK OVERTHROWN BY MUSLIM BROTHERHOOD

1995-1996

KEMP LOSES NOMINATION TO POWELL
OPERATION DESERT SHIELD-II OVER
SOLAR POWER REPLACES OIL IN 50% OF CALIFORNIA OFFICES

LIMITED SDI SYSTEM OPERATIVE
SECOND IRISH STATE CREATED
GERMAN-POLISH BORDER VIOLENCE ESCALATES
THOUSANDS VISIT AS MUNICH NAZI MUSEUM OPENS
EUROPE CLOSES BORDERS TO RUSSIAN MIGRANTS
ROMANIAN CROWDS CHEER SOCIALISTS
HITLER BUNKER MUSEUM OPENS

HONG KONG COUNCIL REJECTS SINO-BRITISH ACCORDS

KOREAN UNIFICATION TALKS CONCLUDE WITH PACT
TAIWAN SEEKS RECOGNITION AS COUNTRY
U.S.-JAPAN FREE TRADE AGREEMENT SIGNED

BLACK MAJORITY OPENS PARLIAMENT IN CAPETOWN
U.S. ENDS ISRAELI AID

GENETICALLY ENGINEERED FUNGUS WIPES OUT POPPY
AIDS VACCINATION DISCOVERED
WORLD REFUGEE POPULATION TOPS 40 MILLION

As some of these headlines suggest, a new world disorder is immediately ahead. The breakdown of the Soviet state and its regional hegemony is already giving rise to long-repressed nationalism of the nastiest sort in Eastern Europe. Self-determination in some countries has proven to be highly divisive, as ethnic groups vie with each other for territory and the "right" to exclude outsiders. But the conflicts such struggles will produce are not likely to be as long lasting as those of the cold war era, although they may be bloodier. By the mid-1990s, the fate of newly liberated nations and the old empires that controlled them will largely be determined. Much the same will happen with those interstate conflicts of long standing in the Middle East. The declining salience of the cold war-era military alliances in that region, coupled with the eroding ability of the superpowers to finance and enforce a balance of power globally, will produce uncertainty and upheaval over the short to medium term. In the process, the map of the modern world will certainly change in this region as well.

Within 1991 alone, the stories behind many of these headlines began to be written. For example, two states went out of business: the German Democratic Republic and the Union of Soviet Socialist Republics. Elsewhere,

- The two Koreas took important steps toward ending decades of hostility and making it possible for leaders in the north and the south to talk meaningfully about unification and the denuclearization of their peninsula.
- The opposing forces in Northern Ireland began an equally novel and significant dialogue with Great Britain.
- Israel recognized the Palestinians as an entity with which the Jewish state must negotiate over self-determination.
- At one time or another during the year, leaders in virtually every state noted the degree to which they were losing effective sovereignty over their economies as the communication systems and technology of interdependence steadily created a borderless trading world.

With the possible exception of the period when the Roman Empire was created or the fifty years of European reorganization and colonization from 1868 to 1919, consequently, there has never been more flux in the nature of sovereignty in the international system. I have chosen to characterize what is happening, in fact, as foreshadowing the erosion of sovereignty—something that was inevitable as interdependence grew and that is largely desirable for the future.

The present erosion of sovereignty has not occurred because of the defeat of any major power in a shooting war or the rearrangement of the international system due to the rise of regional or global hegemons. The process, in other words, has not been a zero-sum game, and it has not occurred in ways that have been detrimental to basic human rights and needs.

Instead, the modern state today is part of an ever-expanding network of trading regimes and networks that enhance the ability of its citizens to receive goods and information from everywhere. Central governments are less and less able to prevent such transactions. The other key aspect to what is happening is the degree to which we have voluntarily arrived at the erosion of sovereignty. Consider, for example, the steps an increasing number of governments have taken to control and eliminate the use of substances and products that have adverse effects on the environment. There is no longer much, if any, dispute over the need to cooperate on a global basis to eliminate the use of chemicals known to deplete stratospheric ozone, to monitor and reduce the production of greenhouse gases, to conserve tropical rain forests, to cease hunting and netting practices that threaten species diversity, and to dispose of toxic wastes safely. A decade ago, powerful political forces could be mustered in many countries to block or forestall regulations and limitations that would adversely affect the interests of those who gained from environmental pollution and animal cruelty. One of the chief arguments used in that era was the need to assure national sovereignty and to protect it from the application of global norms and practices. But today, people virtually everywhere accept the need to end agricultural, animal husbandry, and manufacturing practices that threaten the environment.

What has not yet eroded are the very sharp distinctions people and nations draw between themselves and others. The trend toward democratization, especially in Eastern Europe, has brought with it the demand by numerous ethnic groups for self-determination, and this in turn has been accompanied by considerable upheaval and violence over when and how this should happen. In large as well as small multicultural states particularly, the center— that is, the confederal arrangement to govern disparate ethnic and social groups in such a way as to make them obey the will of a centralized authority— has not held. But what is most interesting about this phenomenon from the perspective of sovereignty is that the new entities being created seem as willing as those they replaced to accept the erosion of sovereignty described above. Not a single new state has sought to renege on international treaty obligations to protect the environment, and some—as in the case of the new commonwealth among some of the republics of the former Soviet Union—have agreed to begin a process of regional integration modeled after the European Community.

By early in the twenty-first century, I suspect that the process everywhere will have gone far enough to cause a substantial revision of the charter of the United Nations. The General Assembly will no longer operate on the basis of individual nations voting but through regional assemblies and working groups. The permanent members of the Security Council will no longer have their veto power, which will allow the body to take binding actions by majority decision. U.N. peacekeeping forces will be reconfigured in order to be able to be deployed in peacemaking roles, and the International Court of Justice will have won the Nobel Peace Prize for its work in boundary and border dispute resolution. The U.N. specialized agencies will become both more powerful and more central to the administration of certain global norms and rules relating to the conservation of the environment, the treatment of refugees and immigrants, the health and welfare of children, and the prevention of the proliferation and transfer of weapons.

If this occurs as I forecast, what sense of power will the presidents of the United States and the United States of Europe have? They will still be at the heads of very important and powerful organizations whose actions will greatly affect international issues and problems. But they will have much less of a sense that their decisions and policies will determine how those issues are resolved. They will govern societies with great impact on the lives of people in many other countries, and they will work on problems many other leaders will have an interest in resolving. Above all, they will have a commitment to maintaining a stable and open international system—as opposed to one they are able to effectively control and manipulate for unilateral advantage—in which goods, services, people, and ideas can move continually and freely as opportunities present themselves.

In sum, a profound transformation lies ahead even for well-established powers. Some change will occur in the wake of internal political, ethnic, and religious upheavals, which may prompt the subsequent division of even more countries, and this process may be very violent. Other violence may be caused by extremists who will resist the settlement of long-standing disputes (in Korea, Israel-Palestine, Northern Ireland) the closer these disputes actually get to being settled.

But such upheaval will hasten another and offsetting trend: The greatest amount of change in world politics will result from the regional integration in Europe and elsewhere.

Over the longer term, it is the phenomenon of integration rather than fragmentation that will hold the most significance for the international system and the organizations that manage it. The forging of economic and then political unions that do for many states that which can be done by none alone will be the way the next generation of world leaders achieves security, legitimacy, and prosperity. In the process, democracy will become practically universal as a form of governance because it is only through free choice that people share what they have in the hope of improving the future for all.

If these developments are what we in the United States want to have happen, a strategic vision about how to achieve them will be particularly important in coping with and countering the coming upheaval. As this book will show, there is presently a disconnect between what today's leaders know how to do and what the future will need for them to do. From Russia to America, leaders are required who have the vision and skill to preside over the dismantling of enormous defense industrial complexes in ways that do not further depress their economies and through which new jobs can be created into which those formerly associated with defense and military spending can be redeployed. New economic plans are needed to assure that peace dividends accrue and then are wisely spent. New social and political arrangements need to be constructed that allow much more extensive and active political participation and yet also enable governments to make the decisions that will enable free markets to exist at all levels. These challenges will also require a U.S. foreign policy that in the medium term demonstrates the following:

- A firm commitment to the success of democratization by all of the members of the Commonwealth of Independent States that replaced the U.S.S.R., the creation of a multilateral "Marshall Plan" program to promote the transformation of the economies and political systems of formerly socialist and Communist countries on a global basis, and the effective linking of Japan to all that is happening.
- An equally firm and multilateral commitment to work to attract and integrate the states that are currently outliers to the transformation of the international system: Iran, Iraq, North Korea, Cuba, Libya, and especially China. Dealing with these states will involve creating the conditions under which their leaders will see it in their own best interest to renounce the use of force, the acquisition of additional nuclear and other advanced military capabilities, and the export of revolution and to participate in international relationships based on the rule of law and adherence to the Universal Declaration of Human Rights.
- Multilateral pursuit of the resolution of conflicts stemming from the colonial and cold war eras, especially in the Middle East, South Asia, and Africa. This will involve recognition of the fact that the denouement of the Gulf and Angolan wars, the ending of apartheid, and the Arab-Israeli peace talks represent historic opportunities for more effective U.S. involvement in international affairs as part of a concert of countries engaged in promoting conflict resolution.
- Such international conflict resolution will also require U.S. modesty and involve the United Nations and its secretary-general in an increasingly forward posture as a peacemaker rather than as solely a peacekeeper. This will require U.S. support for an increase in the political, technical, and financial resources available to the world body for such activities and for an increase in the permanent membership of the U.N. Security Council. The United States should also support putting the U.N. system as a whole on sounder financial terms as its specialized agencies take on greater responsibility for managing the global regimes concerned with the preservation of the environment.

For the next century our aim should be to create an international system capable of managing itself and in which the primary actors in world politics may not even be states. In an era of crosscutting global issues combined with regional and functional alignments, aggregations of countries based on common currencies and markets—or entirely new ones based on ethnic affinities rather than a distinctive political order—could become the principal units of action in international affairs. Some of these units could grow out of presently existing institutions, such as the European Community (EC), and continue to expand. Others could arise as changing national boundaries (for example, in the former Soviet Union and the Middle East) create smaller but more coherent states. In order to function effectively and become viable entities, these states would be compelled to enter into some form of economic (at least) and political confederation. Yet other international institutions could be formed as nations search increasingly for a more effective vehicle to tackle such key global issues as ozone depletion, migration and refugee problems, the destruction of tropical rain forests, the transmission of AIDS and other plague-like diseases, and the proliferation of weapons of mass destruction. As a result of such global transformations, membership and voting arrangements in the U.N. General Assembly will also have to be revised. When this happens, many nation-states as we know them will be superseded as the principal unit of accounting for power or principle in international affairs.

In such a "postnational" order, decisionmaking will be much more complex and probably initially far more uncertain than it is today. As new regional and global centers of authority emerge, new processes of reaching and enforcing decisions will have to be developed as ethnic groups, economic organizations, and political forces participate essentially as coequals—or functional equivalents—in resolving questions that, it turns out, affect them all. This will involve developing a concept of democracy of perhaps a very different sort than the kind with which we are familiar today. Some of those making decisions will not be popularly elected and yet their interest will have to be respected, whereas others will have to be consulted and included despite what may be very different cultural outlooks on the degree to which decisions should reflect any degree of popular participation. There is, consequently, a danger that in its early institutional forms, the need for a new order will outstrip the ability of people generally to feel comfortable with how it works or to relate it to the ideologies on which they have been raised. This is why it is so important for the principal actors in such a system to think now about how it should be organized and what they would like to see it represent and accomplish.

As daunting as that task may presently seem, it is crucial to remember that the era that began in 1989, is probably the first time in history that so many leaders have had a role in outlining the shape of a new world order. This is also the first time in the twentieth century that so many leaders of key nations, including the military superpowers, subscribe to the view that a system of world order should be based on the peaceful settlement of disputes, resistance against aggression, the control and reduction of arms, and the promotion of human rights. These are values an increasing number of nations now share, which suggests that the construction of the future world order can be done with a degree of harmony and coordination hitherto unimaginable. And therein lies the key to assuring that this time, and for the new century ahead, the history of the future will be substantially different—and in most respects, better—than the past.

3

The Impact of the Idea of Freedom

Shortly before his death in 1976, Chinese premier Chou En Lai was asked by a French journalist for his opinion of the impact of the French Revolution on world politics. Chou replied, "It is too soon to tell." Much the same should be said about the impact of what has come to be called the trend toward democratization taking place on virtually a global scale today. For the simple fact is that we still don't fully comprehend the power and majesty of the idea of freedom, as well as the degree to which people who have never been free and who do not fully understand freedom's consequences take enormous risks to become free.

Throughout this book, I use the terms "freedom" and "democratization" in close relationship to each other.

Freedom is the idea that all people have equal dignity and rights that entitle them to think and act according to their own will and for their own good, as long as their actions do not harm others. Democratization is the process by which people have increasingly come to maintain freedom. It involves the expansion of political participation, the creation of new organizations and systems to assure channels of representation and the right to redress for hitherto excluded and powerless groups, and the establishment of individual and institutional safeguards (usually through the strengthening of legal systems) to assure that such participation and the making of such claims can be provided for citizens without fear of reprisal. Methods of accomplishing each of these elements of a democratic political system can and will vary from place to place and over time. Prior to the events of 1989-1990, it was already evident that many forms of democracy were feasible and that numerous political, economic, and legal roads to achieving democratization were available. For example, the United States, France, and Israel all view themselves as democracies. Yet, their governments and legal systems function very differently, and the process by which groups are empowered and make their demands known in each country is vastly different. So, too, are the expectations of people in each of these countries with respect to their political rights and privileges and their views of the degree to which government should intervene to assure that all have access to power and that all abide by the decisions made by those currently in power.

Right now, of course, political scientists and social philosophers are very much focused on defining the particular features of and routes toward democratization that function most efficiently in specific types of situations. Hence, no universal recipe can be applied to aid the countries of Eastern Europe, the former Soviet Union, and the newly industrializing and democratizing countries of Asia, Latin America, Africa, and the Middle East. Instead, a bewildering variety of public and private missions and groups from the established democracies has sought to provide direct technical assistance and establish joint economic ventures with their counterparts. Nevertheless, some common threads have emerged:

- Democratization cannot progress very far without corresponding economic reform and change that enable governments to deliver on the promises about freedom making people's lives (versus just their political system) better.
- Toleration of differences of all sorts (political, ethnic, religious), as well as of the processes and the outcomes by which trade-offs among them are achieved, is also essential. People must learn to accept the fact that decisions within a democracy are reached through communication and compromise. If individuals are critical of each other's proposed solutions to current problems—and lose elections over them—then this is part of the process rather than the occasion for a coup or for withdrawal from the arrangements that brought them to power or provided them with a share of the power in the first place.
- Formal constitutional confirmation of basic rights—speech, religion, press, assembly, and enterprise—must be established in order to provide an institutional framework and guarantee an environment of liberal information exchange and acceptance of social diversity. Clear laws are then needed to protect the freedom of political participation and the right of the entrepreneur to make a profit, as well as to dispose of that profit in a manner dictated by his or her own self-interest. Those who have a dispute to bring to a court of law, moreover, must be confident that their arguments will receive a fair and independent hearing.

None of this advice assures that democracy will take root in all situations, as I suggest later. But in the 1990s and beyond, there is no doubt that the defining issue of world and national politics will be the degree to which freedom can be fostered, democracy tailored to local conditions and requirements, and then governmental systems reformed.

Although the move toward democratization will involve the steady expansion of political participation and the globalization of human rights, the degree of freedom associated with governments and economic systems established in its wake may increase at different rates. Clearly, it would be desirable to have transitions to free markets and free political systems occur simultaneously or in some tandem fashion so the expectations generated by one system do not outrun the capacity of the other to provide them. However, most societies now undergoing change lack the human and economic resources to achieve both wealth and freedom at the same time. For the foreseeable future, consequently, we will encounter situations in which political participation will initially expand at far greater rates than economic growth, and this evolution will likely generate essentially free market economic systems in the midst of polities that are only partly free. As a result, some situations lie ahead in which the backlash effect of stalled economic growth and the emotional anxieties over anticipated dislocations and inequities, which may result from the sudden withdrawal from centrally planned economies, will cause temporary halts in and even reversals of governmental change and political reform. Some societies will voluntarily choose prosperity over freedom, as has been the case in such countries as Singapore and until recently Taiwan and South Korea, but few will be able to do so indefinitely.

The point is that we should be prepared for the variety of individual ways in which countries move toward democracy. In response to these developments, our notion of the types of governments that may potentially exist will have to adjust and evolve well beyond the original paradigms and conceptions formed in the wake of the great revolutions and changes of the late eighteenth century. Within this transforming environment, political philosophers will fulfill an important role in imagining the future. They will help practitioners to understand the importance of allowing the core values that underlie the process of democratization to reform and define the most effective and appropriate institutions for a given society.

Freedom and Upheaval

The history of the future begins with the idea of freedom. In recent years, we have seen an unusually large and increasing number of people (mostly unnamed) defy and topple governments and systems in which no freedom was permitted. We have been mesmerized by the courage of individuals who, for example, step out of a crowd in China's Tiananmen Square and bring a column of army tanks to a halt. We have been intrigued by the mystery of what was going on in that individual's mind and why the driver of the tank stopped. Did both understand the consequences of their actions? And did the heroic act of resistance succeed at that moment because of the power and appeal of the idea behind it? We will probably never know for sure. But what occurred that day in June 1989 irreversibly changed China and many other countries forever. It did not, of course, bring immediate freedom; however, it created a symbol and established a precedent that will someday bring freedom. This isolated act of courage also led others, like Russian president Boris Yeltsin, to imitate the act in hope of repeating at least the immediate effect.

We have long been aware of the power of symbols, like flags and statues, to motivate people to make sacrifices or inspire them to expose themselves to personal risk for some greater good or noble objective. What is unusual about recent events is that for the period 1945-1985, the symbols to which people had responded represented and promoted systems of dictatorship rather than freedom.

There is scarcely a dictator left today, however, who can remain isolated from the global trend toward freedom. Many are finding that they are unable to inspire popular support or to suppress effectively political or economic choices that are different from those the regime has dictated. Unfortunately, some incumbents will continue to try, and they will persist in seeking to gain power in order to create advantages for their group, clan, or class at the expense of others. None of these efforts is likely to prove successful over the long term, and this is a fundamental difference between the age we are entering and the one we have just left. Previously, it was the dictator and not the democrat who was likely to gain power and hold it longer. Why?

When Philippine president Aquino coined the term "people power," she was in the midst of a struggle against one of the world's most well-entrenched despots, who commanded both a large army and substantial wealth. She had few advantages: Her assassinated husband was the one who had possessed the marriage's political savvy and negotiating skills; she did not have the support of the U.S. government (which, if it tilted at all in the early days of the Philippine Revolution, did so by veering toward neutrality); and she was unsure of the degree to which the Roman Catholic church hierarchy would support her if she claimed to be the legal winner of a national election. Surely, Aquino would have been skeptical of church objectivity had she viewed the films showing Cardinal Sin and other high church officials in attendance at Marcos family birthday parties and the New Year's Eve celebrations in 1986.

But Aquino managed to sense and tap a potentially much more powerful and fundamental force at work in the streets, churches, and army barracks. In its most elemental form, people power is a synergy of ideas and actions. It incorporated perceptions of fairness and expectations of responsible government and translated these ideas into actions during occasions when opportunities arose for people to demonstrate their courage and to risk their own lives and careers in order to gain a better life for their family and the future of their country. Such power, it turns out, does not arise from prolonged study or reflection on the classic works about freedom written by ancient political philosophers. In addition, it does not sprout entirely from observing examples of free political systems operating successfully in other parts of the globe. Instead, it materializes with breathtaking speed and is conveyed by modern (e.g., the fax) and antique (primarily radio) communications systems alike. Its premises are simple and easily understood by persons who have never left the towns and villages where they were born, whose homes have no running water or electricity, and who may not even be able to read or write. But the idea of freedom—the idea that people can be free of the repression that comes from corrupt local policemen and from poverty, the promise that this will one day mean a better life, if not for them, then for their children—gets through, and without the endless meetings and infrastructure required to explain and build support for socialism.

A popular desire for individual freedom acted as a catalyst to bring about the collapse of communism in the former Soviet republics and Eastern Europe. During a World Economic Forum in Switzerland on 4 February 1992, Vaclav Havel, then president of Czechoslovakia, observed that "communism was not defeated by military force but by life, by the human spirit, by conscience, by the resistance of Being and man to manipulation. It was defeated by a revolt of color, authenticity, history in all its variety, and human individuality against imprisonment within a uniform ideology."

The nature of crowds—something well studied by social scientists and most feared by socialists and dictators—is also directly linked to the inevitable triumph of people power. The dictators who fell in the 1980s were toppled mainly by excited crowds that stormed palaces, held back troops, or prevented troops from firing at unarmed civilians. These crowds then continued to turn out in support of those leaders who offered the hope that all could be free. Previously, most dictators were removed by coups within the top levels of government. Powerful cabals composed of small groups of hostile military or political associates traditionally staged the revolt and assumed power. Today, dictators are removed more often by anonymous crowds and swells of insurrection from below.

So, it is interesting to imagine the varieties of thoughts and emotions running through the heads of the individuals in the crowds surrounding the Philippine army barracks and attempting to prevent tanks from advancing and dispersing the demonstrations, or in the minds of the people who crammed into trains moving west and climbed over walls to escape Eastern Europe, or the masses who protested for freedom in Derzinsky and Wenceslas squares or the Gdansk shipyard.

Empowerment

Why did so many people gather? What were they trying to achieve? What cost were they ready to pay? And to whom would they look for leadership? At the time, most likely, few demonstrators could offer ready answers to these questions, for quite unlike the crowds that gathered in protest during most of the cold war era, these were not the products of trained Communist subversives or religious fundamentalists. Quite the contrary, those who urged people to gather and who instigated the demonstrations probably did not have the high level of organization and leadership skills for which socialist agitators are legendary. Instead, they had an idea. They imagined that by gathering, people would somehow become freer and that a taste of freedom would inspire them to want more. So, the word was passed by telephone, by copier, by word of mouth, and at church services and labor union meetings that attendance and numbers would be crucial factors in the success or failure of the protest and the quest for freedom. Fortunately, during these popular demonstrations, leaders and bystanders alike shared the idea of freedom; namely, that as citizens, they should be permitted to gather and that the aims the crowds sought were basic rights rather than favors governments should bestow when pressed.

One of the clearest statements and insights into the crowd motivations and mentality came from a professor of philosophy of natural sciences at Moscow State University who found himself drawn to the streets during the August putsch against Gorbachev. As he wrote:

> I was at the Russian White House on the night of August 20-21, from ten in the evening to six in the morning. I stood in one of the human chains of those who guarded, arms locked together, the approaches to the building. . . . First among . . . [my] feelings was an acute sense of the unreality of it all, of the uniqueness and even impossibility of what was going on. The scene there was a combination of an outdoor party and holiday euphoria, with complete indifference to one's own fate. . . The main feeling, in the end was one of liberation. . . the realization of oneself as a human being whose point of view can be changed by the power of persuasion, but not the persuasion of power."[1]

■ **DATELINE MOSCOW**
—Sandra Clemens McMahon

The Russian people finally found a "stage for their action and a voice for their rage." The scene of the confrontation was chaotic yet inspiring, as 150,000 Muscovites in front of the Russian parliament building chanted "We will win!" and citizens fearlessly shouted "Fascist!" or worse at the waiting troops, mockingly scrawled swastikas in the dirt on the tanks, and brazenly climbed aboard armored personnel carriers to argue with the commanders and urge them to retreat. It was obvious that this attitude signaled the end of the fear and of the repressive tactics and threats that had so effectively preserved the former Soviet Union. At Yeltsin's White House, thousands of demonstrators persistently built barricades to deter an attack, supplemented by human chains of unarmed protestors. At the base of the main staircase, an organizer with a megaphone invited, "All courageous men who are willing to defend the building please come forward!!" In response, "About 90 men formed up in three rows on the stairs." Meanwhile, an Orthodox priest in full regalia read the Lord's Prayer to the volunteers. At another site in the square, a line of women defiantly faced the troops, displaying signs that read "Soldiers: Don't shoot mothers and sisters!" In response, military troops were reluctant to fight. According to the driver of a light tank stationed near the Russian parliament building, "I will not shoot at unarmed civilians."

There were apparent generational shifts among the demonstrators: Previous pro-Yeltsin rallies attracted people in their 50s and 60s, while the crowds protecting the White House consisted of protestors mainly in their 20s and 30s. This gathering may be classified as the Soviet consumer generation, which has profited from the experience of six years of glasnost and relaxed social and economic conditions. The members of this generation are currently attached to the concepts of social freedom and making money and are relatively unconcerned with political or ideological considerations. For example, Ilya Reznikov, 23, a student council president at the Russian State University for the Humanities, expressed a typical youthful viewpoint as he explained his personal motivation:

> During the coup, my conscience and beliefs were on one side of the barricades at the Russian parliament, but my party membership card was on the other side. I decided it's better to keep my conscience than my party card. The coup finished the Communist Party, but life will go on. Young Soviets will find new outlets for political activity. It will be a healthy society with healthy youth. We will smoke marijuana, make money. We'll have hippies and Yuppies, just like the rest of the world.

Andrei Kortunov, 34, political analyst at the Soviet Academy of Sciences, offered a similar perspective about the primary interests of the youthful crowd. He observed that "a new generation of Russians has emerged which no longer fears the government." The individuals defending the barricades, who were generally young—in their 20s and 30s—were not simply protecting Yeltsin and the theory of democracy but were preserving their life-styles, careers, property, and their right to refuse further political obligations. According to Kortunov, "They were there to defend a civilized society rather than any abstract political idea. And that is why they were ready to fight to the end."

The glasnost-inspired economic and social aspirations of the youthful crowds provided the incentive for the demonstrations; however, the establishment of independent power centers within the Soviet system provided the vehicle for mobilization and communication. Since the advent of perestroika, elected officials, independent journalists, and communications entrepreneurs have emerged within the Russian society. The coup leaders were surprised to discover that the Russians have irrevocably entered the information age. They mistakenly relied on popular indifference and public ignorance to assure the success of their political coup. Inevitably, the coup failed because the public was not indifferent or ignorant.

Several facets of the modern technological means of communication remained operative during the coup, as the coup leaders chose to occupy only telephone, radio, and television centers and to close independent newspapers. Unfortunately, they chose to ignore the vital sources of electric power, which operate fax and photocopy machines, and soon realized that they could not stifle the numerous initiatives of domestic and foreign journalists and radio stations to broadcast the events to a Soviet audience of 50 million. In the end, modern communications provided a source of information and organization and proved instrumental in the triumph of enterprising youth over archaic bureaucrats.

—Compiled from the following reports: Kenneth Auchincloss, "Falling Idols," *Newsweek* (2 September 1991), pp. 26, 27 and 51; *Time* (2 September 1991), "The Russian Revolution," Lance Morrow, p. 20, "The Silent Guns of August," Richard Lacayo, p. 31, "Anatomy of a Coup," George J. Church, pp. 35, 38, 39, and 43.

■

The act of gathering took enormous courage. The outcome was uncertain, the action for most of the participants was unprecedented, and for many, there was no clear view as to what subsequent actions or paths should be pursued. Yet, when the situation required it, many participated repeatedly. And the farther they progressed without being arrested, the more empowered they began to feel.

Now empowerment is a term frequently used in America to describe the creative energy that companies should encourage and nurture in the workplace. Empowered employees, it is argued, will make a better product and will stay attentive at the job longer. If encouraged, they will take risks in the hope of creating an opportunity for the company to profit—and thereby increase compensation to some or to all. I think that many of the same thoughts must have passed through the minds of the individuals in the early crowds that generated people power, although they had probably never heard of the term "empowerment." At its most fundamental level, the idea of freedom implies that individual action makes a difference (or should) and that this difference should ultimately matter to others.

When the yearning for freedom ignites a crowd, the result is especially potent, though still poorly understood. Despite enormous volumes of social science literature on crowd behavior and the nature and dynamics of "grass-roots" social movements, we are usually surprised when groups of unrelated individuals riot, protest, or unite to demand rights and powers that have traditionally belonged to a privileged few. But when people are inspired to demand freedom, the results are far more long-lasting and powerful than those of protests or actions generally undertaken in the name of other abstract principles. For although it may take many years to perfect, the idea of freedom immediately empowers people by suggesting that the future can not only be different as a result of their actions, but also genuinely better.

The Fall of Soviet Communism

This conception of freedom is essential to understanding the speed with which the Soviet Union collapsed. We have never before seen a large and complex state and political system fall apart so quickly and for reasons related so directly and immediately to the idea of freedom. The events that toppled the Soviet government and destroyed the Communist party occurred essentially within a six-month period; they did, of course, have roots in events and developments that took place over the much longer period in which perestroika was gradually introduced into the Soviet system.

However, what is important to remember is that the processes created and the groups empowered by the ascent of Gorbachev and his policies of economic and political reform were not designed to inspire such dramatic changes or to end socialism in the country. Virtually no one foresaw what did occur. Even Eduard Shevardnadze, who had warned against a reactionary coup, did not imagine that such a coup would lead to the end of the contemporary Soviet system. He was simply trying to improve and reform the system.

In view of the magnitude of recent developments, it is worthwhile to pause a moment in contemplating the future and to draw some tentative lessons about the events of an extraordinary present.

First, the decline and fall of the Soviet state under Gorbachev is not predominantly a story of corrupt and inept leadership. Although it is clear in retrospect that Gorbachev made several mistakes, he was the most able leader yet produced in Russian and Communist party politics. However, he should have acted differently in 1989 and 1990 to hasten genuine perestroika and he should have realized how impossible it was going to be to accomplish his goals for the Soviet state through the vehicle of a revitalized and reformed Communist party.

It also very much remains to be seen whether it is possible to reform and change practices and fundamental attitudes toward such issues as human rights, religious freedom, and entrepreneurship in the countries of the former Soviet Union during the lifetime of the current generation and maybe even its offspring. The pervasive and deep entrenchment of these attitudes was illustrated to me by a colleague who just returned from interviewing workers in several Russian cities. What the workers seemed to resent most were the people who were making profits by providing services, such as transporting goods to market. Although these entrepreneurs provided much-needed transportation services, the workers were resistant to the concept of service-oriented professions and complained that the entrepreneurs charged a high price for their services. The former Soviet state had provided such services in the past, and its disintegration left a dangerous void in the distribution systems. Yet, in the Communist tradition, average citizens still thought in terms of more tangible fruits of labor, and they resented the fact that wages were earned by private middlemen who did not contribute legitimately more often to the economic cycle by growing or making the product. Most of the people interviewed could not understand why they should pay more for something the seller did not have a direct hand in making. They were not willing to reward the initiative that caused the particular good to be brought to market, the risks taken in doing so, and the benefit gained by having access to the product in the first place. Ironically, as a result, store shelves remain barren as food spoils in the farm regions and the Russians cling to their traditional philosophies. Although communism may be dead, the labor theory of value—and probably many other teachings of Karl Marx—are and will continue to prove quite appealing and durable. How new states and systems will be created by and for a people who religiously believed in the values of the old order—as opposed to methods the Communists of their day used to implement them—is far from clear or certain.

Nor is the collapse of the Soviet Union a story of a state suddenly besieged by insurmountable foreign threats or rampant natural or man-made disasters. In the past, even much smaller states have managed to avoid succumbing to total disintegration in the absence of these critical threats and predicaments. What happened to the Soviet Union may be an entirely new phenomenon—and indicative of the process of challenge and change that states may undergo in the period ahead.

Mikhail Gorbachev—and thereby the forces that shaped his thinking and outlook, as well as those that delivered him to power—remains a central but also a mysterious figure in the recent sequence of events and the ultimate Soviet collapse. We do not yet know why he succeeded in his bid to become general-secretary of the Communist party of the Soviet Union or why he launched the reforms that eventually led to his own downfall and the end of the country he led. But the real mystery is why his calculated actions and reforms ultimately led millions of people—and not just Boris Yeltsin—to take extraordinary steps in support of an entirely new political system and the subsequent creation of a new set of countries. We do not know if Gorbachev was essential to this process once it had started, but we are certain that he could not reverse the process when it raced ahead and advanced much further than he intended or thought desirable.

What I am suggesting is that for the first time, we may have witnessed an entirely new means by which the idea of freedom can gain ground, express itself, and yield consequences. Namely, we saw a process by which organized as well as diffused, and empowered as well as disenfranchised social and political forces prevailed simultaneously on leaders at every level for self-determination and during which the self-entrenched forces in the society, which possessed a monopoly on violence and coercion, allowed all this to happen. We have experienced the dawn of a unique and historical phenomenon: We should now want to know why.

Understanding what went on, consequently, should be a central focus of the political science of freedom. This will compel us to break new ground, both conceptually and methodologically. But we should do so with the most pragmatic of intentions in mind. We will want to investigate the process of breakup and state creation in a new world order so we can better anticipate what is going to occur, assist those processes that are in our interest, and prepare to deal with the results. Thus far, we have learned that change occurs much more rapidly and uncontrollably once the means are established to communicate its dimensions. We have also observed that people may heartily embrace the abstract concept of freedom without translating the idea into concrete terms and drafting a functional model of free systems and institutions for their own societies. This in turn could indicate that the process cannot be controlled or stopped once the change is under way and that a period of great experimentation will follow the period of upheaval and change. The outcome of this experimentation will simultaneously alter the size, definition, and scope of countries, the system by which they are governed, and the nature of their economies and the economic activities of their people. As this happens, people need not be threatened or exploited. In fact, the dynamic and central values of the international system in a new world order could well be to advance freedom in all spheres and to preserve a safe global environment for complex interdependence.

The Movement of People and Ideas

Freedom will also shape the future in another key respect. In today's society, there is a growing recognition of the universal right of people to live where they choose and to move freely from one locale to another in the process of doing so. In tomorrow's society, populations will become increasingly mobile. Already, millions of people are migrating annually in search of greater economic opportunity, religious freedom, or ethnic identity and security.

As people move, they bring with them changing conceptions of what constitutes a nation, of who should be included in it, and of how nations should be governed. As people vote with their feet, they redefine political conditions and amplify the stresses and strains on domestic economies. Often the immediate result is to increase the number of people who expect to reap the benefits of freedom while in the short run reducing the capacity of the government to deliver. This problem occurs because the new arrivals need time to put down roots and become established in ways that allow them to contribute to the economic resource base on which the government can draw. But the key point to remember is that the marginalization and dependencies the new arrivals represent need not be permanent. Eventually, they contribute to the growth and expansion of the resource base and tend to give back to society far more than they originally took. Government policy, therefore, needs to be fashioned and framed in such a manner that it assures recognition of the long-term benefits afforded by such freedom of migration. Such a farsighted policy approach will require resisting demagogic appeals to discriminate against migrants and nationalistic pressure to close borders, especially newly created ones.

The population shifts of the types described above—coupled with their scale and the multiplier effect, which occurs when one group of people receives information revealing that other groups are able to move freely about the globe—thus will contribute to changing political dynamics in every type of society. In some, this will enable large minority groups to gain access to greater power and top national-level positions. In others, the volume and pace of migration will cause tension and create efforts to prevent the translation of numbers and differential birthrates into political representation and, ultimately, power.

The issues of who is a citizen and of what country will take on greater significance—and cause more turmoil and debate—until population shifts begin to slow and national boundaries and identities become clearer. Eventually, in most situations pressure will emerge to create stability and safeguards for the coexistence of all groups as the preferred alternative to racial tension and ethnic violence. This will allow the new populations to make a greater commitment to their new surroundings and contribute positively to economic growth. By the early 2000s, particularly as world trade becomes more regionalized and common markets proliferate, ethnically diverse societies will become much more stable and effectively governed. On the other hand, those that have consciously chosen to remain homogeneous will also enjoy the benefits and prosper from increasing access to the richness—culturally and economically—of other societies. In the past, the largest source of instability has been resistance to the free movement of people rather than the processes by which they choose to become acculturated or coopted or to preserve their identity in a new location while maintaining opportunities to increase their economic power and political status.

By the middle of the twenty-first century, individuals and groups may be able to move their home and work locations with very little restriction. They will do so based on their skills or educational backgrounds, on where they can find work and succor, and on the information they receive about how to initiate the process. Transportation—even over very long distances—will cost far less in the next century than in this one, and the premium that was paid to smugglers in order to facilitate illegal immigration will become obsolete. This will facilitate seasonal shifts of agrarian labor forces, for example, without the attendant fear that allowing such people to work will often translate into a permanent resident status in the places where they find temporary employment. It will also allow people greater access to education and technology, along with the chance to bring back what they learn to benefit their native society. The ability to move freely, as well as the increasingly lower costs of doing so, will help reverse a half century of brain drain. With the advent of more global options for employment and more flexibility of movement in the work force, scientists and technical experts will become freer and more inclined to live in their native land, with options available to pursue a variety of global travel opportunities through association with multinational organizations or corporations.

Central to the success of national policies, which fully embrace the principle of free movement, is political freedom. In the twentieth century, the people who could afford to move but who have chosen not to return to their native societies have hesitated largely because of the fear that once home, they would risk living in conditions of limited political freedom, little chance of equal protection under law, and greater instability. But even now there are signs that a broad range of people are ready and willing to return to their homelands as political systems are democratized. In this respect, the experiences of Taiwan and Korea in attracting expatriates back from their temporary refuge in the United States and Europe are instructive. These reverse brain-drain programs started in the late 1970s and in the first years showed little sign of success. The programs have now lured back thousands of families, who are making a variety of significant contributions—medical, scientific, management, service, and labor—to society. Clearly, the essential condition for the success of these programs in attracting many vital categories of skilled and talented people was their increasing ability to deliver on the promise that the native societies to which people were returning were becoming freer. Consequently, in the period ahead, the shifting of populations and the liberal movement of people are likely to reinforce the trend toward democratization.

Freedom is, thus, a global phenomenon. Democratization has now occurred on every continent. More countries are free today than at any time in modern history. Although the memory of the fall of the Berlin Wall and the events surrounding it in the Eastern European countries is the image of freedom that most readily comes to mind, the events in central Europe are not isolated. Half of Africa's countries are now governed democratically, a proportion that would have seemed unthinkable just a few years ago. Furthermore, by 1990 all the countries of South and Central America had functioning democracies, and three-quarters of the countries in Asia and a third of the Middle Eastern countries were developing features of democratic political systems.

Not everyone today is free or is living under political systems that have been liberated or democratized by the events of 1989-1990. The cases of China, Cuba, North Korea, Vietnam come readily to mind as examples of entrenched and untouched autocracy. In these societies, more than a billion people are still ruled by Leninist systems. But it is also appropriate to ask: How much longer? By the end of the 1990s, there is a very real prospect that the Communist party elite in each of these countries will be replaced by those ready to practice their own form of perestroika. On an international level, these remaining Communist nations risk becoming further isolated from the world community and their former allies as their numbers steadily decline, their ideological appeal fades, and their economic leverage crumbles. Vietnam has already undergone a power succession that is elevating to positions of top authority a group of leaders seemingly committed to normalizing relations with the United States, integrating Vietnam economically into the world financial system, and allowing the reintroduction of free market systems to help with national development.

The transition to free markets and freer political systems in these countries will be hastened by a combination of domestic factors and international developments. But it will also succeed because the events of 1989-1990 have exposed people, even in these isolated countries, to the idea of freedom and with it, the possibility of change. In the near future, there is probably little we can do to assist and promote the forces that have already been unleashed in these societies; in fact, to identify any such forces prematurely may precipitate a political backlash and become counterproductive. Consequently, our role will be one of preparation. The United States should prepare policies and responses now that when appropriate, will transform the last of the Communist states into republics with genuine freedom in the future.

Democratization and American International Interests

What benefits the United States derives from promoting democratization, and how we can best accomplish this goal still requires considerable thought.

Clearly, in the past we have elected to establish relationships with dictators and in some circumstances, have actually preferred working with the autocrats rather than with their freedom-loving but virulently anti-American counterparts. Even recently we have not initially been entirely comfortable with those leaders who have emerged in the wake of democratization movements in Eastern Europe and the former Soviet Union. Less than a year before his election to the Russian presidency, for example, Boris Yeltsin was thought to be a demagogue and far less desirable a leader, from the U.S. viewpoint, than Mikhail Gorbachev. Despite the events in Tiananmen Square in 1989, the Bush administration opted to avoid distancing itself from China's leaders. So, even though we applaud the trend toward democratization everywhere, its impact on U.S. interests and policies is far from clear.

What will it mean to live and work in a far more democratized and changing world order? This is the key question we should be confronting for long-term strategic planning. Preoccupation with questions of personnel rotation and of who right now is likely to succeed whom in the countries undergoing economic transformations and political change is superficial. Eventually, all national leaders will be forced to manage the popular demands for freedom and, for their own survival, to offer concessions or reform.

I adopt as my starting point the conviction that democratic politics in the period ahead will be messy and unpredictable. Because they reflect the expansion of political participation and the growth of demands on government, such politics will produce situations in which expectations rise far faster than they can be fulfilled. Popular disappointment will lead to electoral defeat and regime change. To stave off defeat, democratic politics in this period will spawn demagogues, separatists, racists, and scapegoaters—pathologies that are to be deplored but that are difficult to eliminate in truly democratic political systems, where the measure of freedom is the guarantee of equal expression for all types of views and where all factional leaders are free to compete for and to gain power.

In less abstract and general terms, this means we are very likely to encounter a variety of political figures who do not share a set of common values or commitments, such as promoting global stability or preserving the type of world order we are presently trying to create. It also means, as we are already observing, that we will see the rise of far more local leaders who think their locality, and the ethnic group it encompasses, should be granted much greater power to govern itself or be permitted to separate and form a country in its own right—possibly with the prerogative to exclude those who are not part of the particular ethnic group that commands a majority. In the process of democratization, many organizational systems will be tested, and many will fail. Some will be more democratic than others. Eventually, a balanced and responsive structure will be achieved and will survive the test of time. In view of the experiences of the oldest democracies—France, Great Britain, and the

United States—the process will be lengthy. These democratic models have been in existence for over two hundred years and are still experiencing continual political, legal, economic, and social reform.

One clear implication is that the use of formal treaty alliances in the future will decline substantially as a pillar of U.S. foreign policy, as economic interdependence and regionalization emerge as the new forces of cohesion and affiliation. So, too, will our ability to rely very heavily on the coordination of economic and foreign policies of the leading industrialized countries as a means of leverage and of shaping the rest of the world in our image. The world of tomorrow simply won't function in that manner, as regional power centers surface in the so-called Third World to compete with and stand apart from the traditional policies of the dominating industrialized powers. This development will compel the United States to conduct its foreign policy through a wide network of relationships and consultations.

The kind of future I envision will also place a premium on staying deeply involved in international affairs. U.S. interests will be much better served if we can anticipate future needs and develop policies that foster the cooperation of a broad range of countries and if our diplomats can prepare the stage by establishing the links and procedures to facilitate such consultation and support. This strategy will take us back into the cloakrooms of the United Nations and requires us to become much more aware of and better represented in the myriad regional organizations that are emerging on the international scene. We can also assure our future position by cautiously, systematically, and comprehensively aligning with and increasing aid to efforts promoting democratic political change. Originally proposed by President Ronald Reagan as a means of competing more effectively with a hostile Soviet Union, the U.S. government involvement in financial and technical support to democratic political parties and labor unions will take on even greater importance and significance in the period ahead. Clearly, we will need to lay the groundwork that identifies us as firm supporters of ventures designed to promote democratic development and change on a global basis. We will also need to be far less hesitant than we have been to date in identifying visibly with democratic political change and helping in the process. Indeed, support for democratic development should have far greater priority in our foreign aid programs and should be the hallmark of a renewed U.S. commitment to internationalism. Although the next century will not be an American one, it can hardly lead to the changed world order we seek without our substantial help and leadership.

Notes

1. Aleksei Barabashev, "In the Human Chain at the White House," *The Woodrow Wilson Center Report* (November 1991), p. 2.

4

The Real Revolution:
Communications and Other
Technologies of Freedom

Our changing world order is also a by-product of the ability to communicate data and ideas across borders, cultures, and time zones using technologies to which virtually everyone has access. The most revolutionary occurrence in the 1980s was the advent and wide distribution of low-cost, effective global communications.

Five minutes of telephone, television, or telex/telefax time cost ten times less to communicate in 1990 than it did in 1980. And it is currently one hundred times easier to relay a message. Changes and improvements have been so radical and communications have become so widely available that it is truly difficult to imagine the conditions of political and economic life before the age of personal computers (PCs), faxes, minicams, and the ability to transmit data and visual images instantaneously across continents.

As a result of these technological advances, the exchange of ideas and values suddenly became possible on a worldwide scale. In 1980, international telephone calls were carried on land lines and undersea cables at great expense and difficulty; in most countries the caller had to make a reservation or face waits of one to three hours to place such a call while operators attempted to locate a free circuit. At the beginning of the decade, only twenty satellites were available for limited international communications. Today, more than thirty satellites orbit the globe, providing a system of reliable, massive, nearly worldwide communications on a twenty-four-hour basis. The average cost of an international telephone call to most foreign countries during the U.S. business day is around a dollar per minute and in many cases a good deal less.

Fortunately, the benefits of the new technology have been widely dispersed. The archaic international dialing procedures of the past decade are standard in fewer than two dozen countries today. From a 1980s communications perspective, it would be difficult to envision a typical morning commute to work in the 1990s as thousands of motorists engage in conversations on their mobile car phones. In fact, the hundreds of thousands of portable cellular telephones currently in circulation make it possible for people on the streets of Hong Kong to receive calls from offices on Wall Street, friends visiting Bahrain, or relatives vacationing in the Bahamas.

The evolution of IBM Corporation products and sales trends is representative of the momentum behind innovations in the technologies that have facilitated global communications. In 1981, IBM began to market its first PC. The machine weighed more than twenty pounds, cost nearly $3,000, and contained 128K of memory. In comparison, the machine I used to write this book approximates a notebook in size and weight, was purchased for half the cost of my first PC, and features a memory measured in megabytes. According to a 1981 announcement by IBM Corporation, its first year's sales of the IBM PC amounted to 10,700 machines; today, Info Corp Consultants estimates there are more than 120 million PC-type computers worldwide. Personal computers exist in every country and have become a necessary instrument in the operation of a majority of businesses, many churches, and even some households.

The same explosive growth has occurred in the realm of fax and telecommunications. In 1980, "send me a fax" meant that a secretary hand-fed a document into a telephone that was set up to look like a Rube Goldberg invention, waited a minimum of five minutes to have the message transmitted, and then spent another half hour calling the recipient to make sure the material had arrived. Fifty percent of the time, the answer was "no," and the process described above had to be repeated. At that time, facsimile machines were novel and quite rare in U.S. business offices, and they cost three to four times what they do today. A modern fax can be purchased for as little as $300 and the total number of fax machines in the world is now in the millions. Over 196,586,000 fax machines were produced in the United States alone in 1991.

What are the implications of having so much information so freely available? As a result of the wide circulation and refinement of the PC and the fax, world politics has been increasingly democratized. The distribution of information about democratic political systems and free markets can no longer be entirely restricted by powerful leaders. As we saw in China during the 1989 prodemocracy demonstrations and the subsequent massacre in Tiananmen Square, most news cannot be suppressed. The constructive impact of unrestricted communications was also evident during the events of the failed Soviet coup in 1991. As the coup unfolded, liberal exchanges of information and data inside and outside the Soviet Union resulted in the unexpected participation of informed domestic and international audiences and contributed greatly to the ultimate failure of the coup. And today, only a handful of truly totalitarian countries exist—for example, North Korea and Libya—in which the leadership can prevent fax machines and computers from falling into unauthorized hands and exposing the leaders' abuses of power.

Television has also drastically changed the democratic character of our world. The ability of television to transport us to worlds we have never seen and places we have never visited, and to introduce the idea of freedom to people who have never experienced it, has created limitless possibilities for educational and political interactions in a global sense.

In recognition of the global achievements and future potential of television broadcasts, the Georgetown School of Foreign Service awarded the 1989 annual Weintal Prize for diplomatic reporting to the Cable News Network (CNN). Ted Turner personally accepted the certificate, one of hundreds I was certain his organization had won. At the reception following the awards, he seemed so genuinely pleased to have been selected as a recipient that I asked him why he valued this particular prize. He replied that this was the first award CNN had received from an institution that specialized in the serious study of international affairs. "Just a year ago," he told me, "people in our industry said that the initials CNN stood for chicken noodle news." "Now," Turner continued, "we are part of the world of international affairs. We can go practically anywhere and will let anyone speak. But the most novel thing is that many more people listen and want to hear news from all over the world." CNN now broadcasts around the clock to over 115 million locations worldwide in over two hundred countries and territories.

We are likely to be overwhelmed from time to time (at best) and overloaded (at worst) with the job of effectively processing the information to which we have access. The average person in an industrialized country today receives about 7 million bits of information a day; this figure will probably double by the end of the 1990s. As anyone who subscribes to a cable television service soon discovers, the technology of information and the low cost of its dissemination have already given us access to far more information than we can possibly absorb. In the near future, we will be able to program the types of shows we wish to watch, those we wish to archive, and those we plan to see simultaneously on split-screen monitors. All personal computers in our homes and offices will also include compact disc (CD) players and local area networking (LAN) as standard equipment by the end of the decade (if not before), providing essentially an encyclopedic base of information for our daily and professional lives and enabling us to tie in to vast networks of data and people. Such networked informational resources will increasingly be available to all persons in all walks of life, from the most sophisticated administrator to the simplest worker. They will be available to doctors making medical diagnoses, to political delegates in legislatures far from home, and to parents struggling to maintain a united family unit. The information will be available at all times as long as there is a reliable source of electrical power for telephone lines or satellite dish receivers. Although we will all spend more for accessible information, rates will be one-ten-thousandth of the cost per bit of information compared to the costs in 1980.

But a central question is whether any of us will be able to use such vast amounts of information more effectively than we do today. Satellites, space vehicles, and telescopes currently transmit huge amounts of information regarding defense intelligence, the environment, and scientific discoveries on a daily basis. The weakest links in the scheme of information collection are still the integrity and effectiveness of the processes responsible for the analysis and communication of the results of new information. As this weakness becomes more evident, some individuals, agencies, or corporations will undoubtedly discover ways to produce more effective analysis and achieve a practical means of communicating the results. There will be people who will appreciate the significance and applications of such comprehensive data bases and access to them and who will translate this information into specific achievements or breakthroughs in the field of politics, business, or science. Much will be accomplished by those who are able to formulate practical applications for new information. Technical analysts and innovators will be able to design uses for such information that others had never considered. Like the computer wizards of the 1980s, these enterprising technicians and inventors will be in high demand, and their skillful use of information, as well as the connections and inferences they are uniquely able to draw, will permanently and constructively change our world.

The Dark Side of the Information and Communications Revolution

The forecast wasn't always so bright. Most social scientists of my generation were trained with reference to theories suggesting that the information and communications revolution sketched above would probably result in repression. As information became more important—that is, more valuable or more damaging to the image of a leader or a regime—a natural tendency would arise to manipulate that information and to manipulate entire populations by playing tricks with both its content and its delivery. Somewhere between the events and developments portrayed in *1984* and *Fahrenheit 451*, we were taught to fear but also to expect a *Brave New World* and not a new world order. The reader, I hope, will forgive my playfulness with these titles—some of which are still banned in local U.S. school systems—which in the 1950s and 1960s shaped our imaginations and convictions and highlighted the negative consequences of the technical achievements of the future. These innovations could lead to political control of the transmission of information. The potential to exert more expansive and tighter control over domestic politics and the daily lives of individuals, especially in those countries governed by Communists and other dictators, was a grave concern of many authors and readers.

These nightmares did not come to pass, and it is doubtful that they are even remotely likely to occur today. On the contrary, the communications revolution and the information explosion have produced consistently positive results. Today, no government—even the most ruthless—has been able to keep information about freedom from all of its citizens, for example. This does not mean such information will cause the remaining dictators to be removed immediately, but it does mean they will become increasingly scrutinized by a global audience and that they have little hope of preventing the broadcast of knowledge about repressive domestic policies and practices from reaching the outside world.

So, the free flow of information around the globe has provided global access to the ideas that make revolutions—and given other less violent forms of political change—and visibility to the motivations promoting these changes and the practical results of such actions. Even though CNN and other television networks have been used by dictators to broadcast lies, they have typically failed to enhance the credibility of those doing the lying. There are simply too many video cameras and too many investigative reporters for the truth to be absolutely suppressed.

Although information makes everyone freer, it does not necessarily make their lives better. In this assessment, George Orwell was right. Writing in 1937, some twelve years before *1984*, in the book *The Road to Wigan Pier* (1958), he found it "queer" to think of "the . . . spectacle of modern electrical science showering miracles upon people with empty bellies." One only has to recall countless newspaper photographs of poverty-level families in homeless shelters and vast public housing projects whose most valued possession is a television set. Even the desperately poor and hungry are able to watch the advertisement of a hundred different life-styles and food products. At times, by glorifying the wealth and rampant consumerism of an elite few, media programming may serve to emphasize the impoverished conditions of the lower socioeconomic classes without offering any type of solution. "Life-styles of the Rich and Famous" or "Dallas" may be extremely depressing programs when viewed by children living in urban tenements. Nevertheless, television allows everyone to dream. Television may also provide inspirational examples or offer educational improvement, as the viewing audience may witness the struggles of poor people in other countries as they discover how to cope with natural disasters or to organize revolutionary groups to seize power from oligarchs in hopes of improving their lives. Without leaving their shelter, the impoverished can receive religious renewal and salvation; attend schools and learn history, math, or languages; or view sporting events whose ticket prices equal collections from months of constant panhandling.

Advances in communications and other technologies will not be welcome by or in all cultures. Indeed, one of the strongest bases for the appeal of today's fundamentalist religions and other conservative social forces is the resistance they offer to change and their indictment of the kinds of change inspired by the free flow of ideas. Not all ideas help maintain the distinctiveness of cultures or the tenure of the elites who govern them. Why might the future be different?

Because of their low cost and the ease with which they can be delivered, the technologies of tomorrow will offer something that has not emerged during the past industrial and other mechanical revolutions. We will witness the distribution of benefits in ways that help the mass of the population to achieve both dignity and basic human needs rather than distributing such benefits largely to those who finance the introduction of technology. If these circumstances evolve, it will be increasingly difficult for even the most fundamentalist regimes to oppose the introduction of technological improvements. In fact, such regimes may find that they are equal beneficiaries of change along with their adherents and that the particular nature and belief systems of their cultures can be maintained more effectively with the aid of technology. It may be counterproductive to oppose the introduction of technology and to take the requisite draconian steps to isolate or ostracize those who would most likely receive its benefits.

Technology and Governance

What will happen as this process unfolds? Will information and communication eventually force governments to deal with empty bellies? And will the documentation of the failure of governments to do so effectively cause them to be overthrown?

Much of the future dynamics is already visible in the domestic conditions within the countries carved out of the territory of the former Soviet Union. Food shortages and long lines are nothing new to Russians and the inhabitants of the republic and commonwealth states. But now, the common hardships associated with daily life—especially those brought on by the lifting of government price controls—are news. Freedom of the press and freedom of speech are indeed new concepts that have inspired a regional communications revolution. Availability of widespread information is helping people to determine and envision what the transition to a free market system means in practical terms, the degree of individual sacrifice required, and the ability of the newly elected governments to develop plans and institutions to cope with the associated shortages and hardships. Access to information simultaneously makes the case of the government easier to make and its performance harder to defend. In order to convince people of the need for sacrifice and of the long-term benefit that will accrue as free markets take hold, the government must speak and act credibly and responsibly. Much as some leaders might wish to do so, there is no way to deny information about how a particular program or reform plan is working while operating under the scrutiny of a free press.

Eventually, the leaders of government will be vulnerable to reelection or removal by the people. And they are now learning that the process of staying in power requires developing practical solutions to current problems and responding to popular demands. Their future, in other words, depends on what the people learn and know about the government's constructive performance rather than on how such information can be controlled and denied.

Western politicians have mastered the art of public relations and election campaigning through the use of mass-media broadcasts and news interviews. They have learned to communicate their leadership qualifications to the general public during prime-time television hours and commercial breaks. In a sense, political leaders have become entertainment personalities—evidenced by the 1980 election of Ronald Reagan, a former Hollywood actor, as president of the United States. But leaders also use the technology of the media to communicate with the public and to bolster support for their programs. They are also subject to much closer scrutiny. In the future, Americans as well as aspiring European, Japanese, and Third World leaders will be forced to adapt even more to the demands of greater openness and accountability.

■ HOW COMMUNICATIONS TECHNOLOGY BROUGHT DEMOCRATIZATION TO POLAND
—Sandra Clemens McMahon

In the wake of the 1981 declaration of martial law in Poland, President Ronald Reagan and Pope John Paul II apparently secretly joined forces to undermine the Polish government and preserve the outlawed Solidarity movement. Initially, they hoped to use Solidarity as a weapon to free Warsaw from Kremlin domination. Ultimately, they hoped to liberate all of Eastern Europe and to accelerate the disintegration of the Communist empire.

When martial law commenced in Poland, communications to the non-Communist outside world were severed, Solidarity leaders were imprisoned, and the union was banned. Under the clandestine guardianship of the president and the pope, Solidarity prospered as an outlaw. Myriad communications equipment was smuggled to the underground organization through channels established by priests, U.S. agents, and representatives of the American Federation of Labor-Congress of Industrial Organizations (AFL-CIO) and European labor unions. The voice of Solidarity was preserved by deliveries of contraband fax machines (the first in Poland), printing presses, transmitters, telephones, shortwave radios, video cameras, photocopiers, telex machines, computers, and word processors. As the resistance matured and established roots, its communications network also afforded unprecedented access to information about the internal decisions of the Polish government and the current topics of Warsaw-Moscow dialogues.

This pragmatic plan was clearly supported in the United States by influential government insiders. According to Zbigniew Brzezinski, national security adviser to President Carter, "This wasn't about spending huge amounts of money. It was about getting the message out and resisting: books, communications, equipment, propaganda, ink and printing presses." Republican congressman Henry Hyde, a former member of the House Intelligence Committee, observed, "In Poland we did all of the things that are done in countries where you want to destabilize a Communist government and strengthen resistance to that. We provided the supplies and technical assistance in terms of clandestine newspapers, broadcasting, propaganda, money, organizational help, and advice. Working outward from Poland, the same kind of resistance was organized in the other Communist countries of Europe."

The state-controlled media and the police forces could not counter the proliferation of independent communications systems. In urban and rural areas, underground newspapers and mimeographed bulletins were circulated and posted, the church published its own newspapers and displayed photocopied Solidarity communiqués on its bulletin boards, and stenciled Solidarity posters adorned most government buildings.

By 1985, it was apparent that Solidarity and its supporters had triumphed. Adrian Karantnycky, who helped organize the AFL-CIO's assistance to Solidarity, reported that by this time, over four hundred underground periodicals were circulating in Poland, with some reaching more than thirty thousand readers. In addition, thousands of subversive books and pamphlets were printed to challenge governmental authority. Even children's comic books were transformed by the underground publishers. They managed to print a new version of Polish fables and legends, which recast the characters and depicted Jaruzelski as the villain, communism as the red dragon, and Walesa as the hero. In addition, millions of Polish families gradually gained access to a mounting supply of documentary videos, which were produced by and played on the contraband Solidarity equipment. Outfitted with modern transmitters and other broadcasting equipment, the union conspirators routinely, preempted the government's radio programming and interjected messages such as "Solidarity lives!" or "resist!" and even interrupted television programming with audio and visual messages that solicited support for strikes and demonstrations. One Vatican official recalled, "There was a great moment at the half time of the national soccer championship. Just as the whistle sounded for the half, a Solidarity Lives! banner went up on the screen, and a tape came on calling for resistance."

Communism collapsed in Poland with shocking speed. By 5 April 1989, both sides signed agreements endorsing the legalization of Solidarity and the introduction of open parliamentary elections in June. Finally, in December 1990, Lech Walesa was elected president of Poland, and the triumph of democracy—nurtured by the technologies of mass communication—was broadcast throughout the global community.

—Compiled from Carl Bernstein, "The Secret Holy Alliance," *Time* (24 February 1992), pp. 28-29, 32-35.

■

Technology and Political Change

No discussion of the forces shaping the international system would be complete without looking into the way in which technology will affect—and change—the nature of the challenges directed at the state. There is no doubt in my mind that technological advances will continue to increase the potential of each person to live a freer and a better life. Individual liberties will be secured to a larger degree as increasing numbers of citizens possess personal instruments of communication and independent access to information. As this happens, the nature of governance will change, as will the expectations of people about what they can provide for themselves versus what they should look to the state to give them. The public will emerge as a consequential and even more outspoken force in politics than it is today. Publics will grow more intolerant of power abuses—directed at social classes, races, gender, children, spouses—as these abuses become more visible. Eventually, instantaneous and widespread exposure of social injustices will create popular pressure to eliminate them and propel society as a whole to protect all citizens. Breakthroughs in basic science, engineering, and the application of technology will also contribute to solving many of the problems that divide us today. Ahead lie vaccines against and cures for cancer and AIDS, the reversal of ozone depletion in the stratosphere and containment of greenhouse gas production, and the discovery of virtually inexhaustible sources of energy completely independent of fossil fuel supplies.

None of us can speak with certainty about how we shall progress from now to then, but we would be foolish to rule out any of these developments. As I started this chapter in the late fall of 1991, for example, European scientists had just announced a major breakthrough in creating and harnessing (if only for a few seconds) the power of nuclear fusion. On 9 November, the huge reactor at the Joint European Torus (JET) project generated a two-second burst of between 1.5 and 2 million watts by an experimental process that involved adding tritium to deuterium atoms. The tritium increased substantially the speed of the nuclear reaction the scientists wanted to create in fusing deuterium atoms, and this in turn led to the release of vast amounts of power approximating the nuclear reactions that take place in stars like our sun. The benefits of this method of generating nuclear energy, when perfected, will be realized in both the low degree of radioactivity expended by the process and its wastes as well as the ease with which the basic ingredients can be manufactured. Both deuterium and tritium can be extracted from water. And some scientists now estimate that through fusion, just two inches of water from the surface of one of the U.S. Great Lakes would generate more energy than burning all presently known fossil fuel reserves.[1]

On 19 November 1991, a Japanese scientist reported the discovery of tubular carbon molecules called fullerenes that if formed into fibers, could create new and far stronger reinforcements for the myriad objects built from polymers. This could result in aircraft wings considerably lighter and stronger than those in use today, for example, and could revolutionize the manufacturing processes that support the transportation industry by increasing the performance of all types of vehicles and substantially improving their safety. Fullerenes are also highly superconductive and transmit electricity at ultra-cold temperatures better than any other material. Suddenly, the carbon we so disparage now as a source of pollution and greenhouse gas could create structures and environments in the future that would require less energy consumption.

What's Ahead?

Science and technology will transform us and the world, as the following suggests:

■   **INVENTIONS/DISCOVERIES THAT WILL IMPROVE**
    LIFE IN THE TWENTY-FIRST CENTURY

—Compiled by Allan E. Goodman, Sandra C. McMahon, and Louis M. Marmon, M.D.

1.   Low-cost desalination processes
2.   Stratospheric ozone regeneration chemicals and manufacturing processes
3.   Holistic diagnostic body scanners that eliminate 99 percent of the need for exploratory surgery

4.   "Safeguard" genetically engineered nucleotides that prevent the growth of cancers and other pathologies and eliminate their transmission from one generation to another
5.   Carbon-composite supersonic transports (SSTs) for intercontinental travel
6.   Computer software generation programs that allow users to specify what they need computers to do while the machines develop the most appropriate and customized solution
7.   Low-cost, portable "Infomen" that connect users to global, real-time data bases
8.   Universal use of computer-based audiovisual teaching machines that allow students to learn basic and applied skills at their own rate and in their own way
9.   Synthetic, disease-free blood plasma
10. Self-replicating fresh-water purifiers that eliminate all waterborne disease
11. Crash-proof, crash-avoiding automobiles
12. Practical, low-cost solar energy generators
13. Automated simultaneous voice and text foreign language translation machines
14. Noninvasive surgical devices and procedures, eliminating 90 percent of the need for anesthesia and incisions.
15. Particle-beam transporters for life-saving medicines and simple organisms.
16. Bacteria-resistant food and animal by-products, eliminating the need for refrigeration of 75 percent of the world's food supply.
17. Self-regenerating oxygen tanks for undersea, high altitude, and space vessels
18. Efficient and low-cost on-site child- and elder-care systems
19. Racial and sexual equality
20. Self-extinguishing flammable chemicals and products so unintended fires will automatically shut down
21. Highly accurate, quarterly weather prediction systems
22. Earthquake prediction and use of peaceful nuclear explosions to redirect the energy of those that will occur
23. Noah's ark
24. A scroll containing an eyewitness account of Jesus' adult life, authenticated to have been written on parchment and with ink at the time he lived
25. The gene that causes murder
26. Environmentally safe nuclear and toxic waste eliminators
27. Dietary treatments that can cure mental illnesses

28. Secure, wealth-generating saving systems to replace compound interest
29. Elements that travel faster than the speed of light
30. How the universe was created and its infinite capacity to expand
31. Why the dinosaurs disappeared
32. The genetic changes and cosmic forces that caused humans to evolve
33. Practical computer memories with the same capability as the human brain
34. Serums to cure learning disabilities and reverse mental retardation
35. Universal health care, with practitioners linked on dedicated, twenty-four-hour global communication networks for diagnosis assistance and consultation on complex diseases and procedures
36. Vaccines to prevent Alzheimer's disease
37. Operation of a U.N. global defensive space shield to protect against terrorist nuclear missile attacks
38. An ethical basis for genetic engineering
39. Widespread applications and use of telepathic communications
40. Construction technologies to create environmentally controlled and pollution-free cities
41. Computerized legal programs used widely to analyze data and prepare final judgments in small claims and misdemeanor violations
42. New propulsion systems and alternate automobile fuels
43. Replenishment of the ozone layer by man-made, space-based lightning bolt generators
44. Computer-piloted commercial airlines
45. Archeological evidence of extraterrestrial visitations to earth
46. Nuclear submarines converted to serve as low-cost satellite launchers
47. Cancer inhibitors and eventual medical cure developed through the concept of directing and strengthening antibodies with injections
48. Earth-based telescopes with capabilities expanded thousands of times through advanced optics and digital computers to explore the boundaries of the galaxy
49. Identity and purpose of the creators of Stonehenge
50. Superconductors used for efficient mass transportation and energy transmission systems

51. Space-based observatories and telescopes to "see" back to within a few seconds of the Big Bang
52. Robotic, responsive artificial limbs
53. Heart muscle tissue regeneration
54. Effective methods developed to extract methane gas from trash dumps
55. Computer arbitration of international labor management and interstate boundary disputes
56. Global use of nuclear fusion to produce electricity
57. Computer replications of the structure and characteristics of the universe discover the existence of a sixth force
58. Computerized drive-through grocery shopping express windows
59. Drug addiction cured through brain stimulation, identification of genes that promote addiction, and dietary control
60. Discoveries in biophysics revolutionize exercise and rehabilitation methods
61. System developed to filter the water and reduce the pollution level of the Mediterranean and rejuvenate other dying seas
62. Interstellar travel and communication
63. Precision-guided pesticides
64. Robots that do all underground mining
65. A renewable energy source
66. A free year of college education for each year of national service
67. Universal high schooling
68. Permanent, individual telephone identification numbers
69. The obsolescence of central business districts
70. The non random nature of pi
71. What happened to *Atlantis*
72. Synthetic spinal cord tissue
73. How to deflect meteors on collision courses with planets
74. Safe fetal surgery for treatment of congenital anomalies
75. Clothing that automatically adjusts to maintain body temperature to fit the environment
76. Computers that communicate exclusively by voice and speech-recognition programs
77. Organ cloning to replace patient's diseased tissue
78. Effective antiviral therapies
79. Safe, effective, and universally available contraceptive techniques
80. Insect-proof and disease-resistant food crops

81. Discoveries in brain research that increase the potential for human "intelligence" development and eliminate learning disabilities
82. Computer-piloted cars that are activated in computer-directed lanes on superhighways and reduce accidents to provide efficient travel options
83. Blending of advanced computers, telecommunications, and consumer electronics to provide universal home access to banking, shopping, education, and cultural events
84. Virtual classrooms replace educational facilities and make college and graduate courses of study available to students regardless of their location and wealth
85. Nonaddictive serums that enhance learning ability and memory capacity
86. Genetically engineered lake algae to neutralize acid rain
87. Vaccines administered to pregnant women for broad-spectrum childhood disease prevention
88. Genetically engineered, rapidly growing "replacement trees" for rain forests and other areas subjected to a high rate of deforestation
89. Forest management techniques and devices that eliminate most naturally caused fires and airborne extinguishers that contain the spread of those caused by negligence and accidents
90. That women make far more effective national political leaders than men
91. Universal firearms ban
92. Universal recycling programs that eliminate fifty percent of waste and refuse
93. Archeological evidence that ends split between Judaism and Christianity over the divinity of Christ
94. Wind turbine generator systems that provide reliable, widespread rural electrification
95. A means to store and convert undersea thermal energy into electricity for coastal cities
96. Genetically engineered bacterium to prevent soil erosion
97. An international real estate transaction law
98. A global corporate taxation system
99. A global currency
100. An intergovernmental system mandating and delivering universal immunizations against childhood diseases

■

We should not imagine the future without anticipating substantial breakthroughs of the types listed above or without thinking that they will indeed improve our relationships with each other and with the planet we inhabit. Consider, for example, the implications of finding an alternate energy source to oil and other fossil fuels and transmitting this power through superconductive lines. The electrification of vast rural and desert areas of the globe would bring people in much closer touch and allow them to tend their lands and herds with far more powerful mechanical aids and efficiency than are even conceivable today. Such electrification could speed the delivery of technical help in eradicating crop diseases and providing medical diagnoses and care. It would also obviate the need to divert waterways and other natural sources of local energy. Regional and national governments could become switchboards for the exchange of technical assistance and other practical forms of help, both within and among countries. The fax and television could provide even the most isolated communities with the range of information currently available only to students and researchers at MIT. Everyone would know how to read and would be aware of the linkage between infant and child death from intestinal disease and the unsanitary disposal of wastes in local water systems.

The century ahead is also likely to prove decisive in humankind's search for understanding how the universe came into being and how it works. It will be a time of dramatic growth in the amount of knowledge about the structure of matter, including that making up our own bodies and the substances which have transmitted plant and animal characteristics over tens of thousands of years. Such knowledge will change the nature of our relationships with all the creatures and phenomena that are part of our planet from one of exploitation to one of conservation because we will see more clearly how our behavior and habits—even at the micro levels—aggregated over hundred of years affect the ability of earth to sustain life. By the twenty-second century, computational techniques and models will be sophisticated enough to forecast the regional impact of human activity fifty to one hundred years into the future. Although these developments will hardly assure that wise decisions are made about development paths, they will contribute substantially to ruling out decisions that have the most serious and damaging results for species diversity and atmospheric pollution.

Hostile clashes with other Third World countries over the environmental cost of the fuels they use to generate electricity would also be reduced considerably by the global dissemination and use of fusion, assuming that its commercial feasibility is eventually proven. To the extent that fusion reactors become available in twenty or more years and replace fission reactors as sources of electrical energy, the potential for production and diversion to weapons use of either highly enriched uranium or isotopic concentrations of plutonium 239 may be reduced, because a pure fusion process necessarily uses neither, and only with unusual modifications could it be made to produce plutonium. Consequently, the likelihood that nuclear reactors in developing states could be used to generate weapons-grade plutonium and other radioactive material necessary for the construction of nuclear bombs and missile warheads would be substantially reduced. And the contribution current methods and the scale of energy production make to carbon dioxide and other so-called greenhouse gas emissions would be reduced to zero within a generation of the appearance of the first fusion plant.

Technology and Tomorrow's Freedoms

Despite the fact that the planet seems threatened now by the technologies produced during the two hundred years of the industrial revolution, by the twenty-first century science may offer a strong opportunity to reduce these threats substantially as well as to improve the conditions of human life. If present trends continue, these developments are likely to create benefits for human life and relationships that far exceed the technological advances of the past five hundred years. In the past, the engine of change has been war. During periods of conflict, technology has been developed to improve the fighting capacity of one monarch, country, or ethnic group. The driving force behind the technology of the future, it seems to me, is much more likely to be peace. Innovation will grow out of the need to make peace between warring ethnic or regional groups and to avoid further conflict over the planet's scarce and clearly hard-pressed basic resources.

No one knows, of course, whether the earth was designed to contain 5 or 6 billion inhabitants. But the more we discover about our collective impact on the planet, the more capable we become of protecting and conserving it. We have also not yet scientifically determined whether the future climate of the earth will be warmer or cooler. The topic of global warming is a significant issue on the agenda of international affairs these days, and virtually everyone has a sense that the earth's climate has gotten hotter and drier since the late 1980s. The causes of the phenomenon are unclear, but the consequences of global warming for food production, coastlines, desertification and deforestation, and population growth and movements are not hard to imagine. Should these forecasts increasingly appear likely, technology will be called on to ameliorate the consequences. This in turn will increase the sense that people possess the potential to master the environment and, in the longer run, to improve their methods of managing the earth.

We should also be prepared for the alternate prospect of global cooling, which I think is much more likely by the years 2030 to 2040. The earth has already exceeded the longest of about twenty-four periods of global warming, as measured by the earth's core and ocean floor sediment samples. Each has lasted about ten thousand years, except for the present Holocene, which is in its eleventh millennium. Conceivably, the use of fossil fuels has prolonged this warm period just as the population has exploded, requiring longer growing seasons and larger harvests. Should the Holocene end and world temperatures drop 5 to 10 degrees Fahrenheit, technology and international cooperation will be no less important to finding a way to cope with this development.

Nevertheless, in the case of either prospect, the relationship between people and governments will change. As communities and ethnic groups are affected by global temperature changes, they will expect more from government. They may also demand a larger share of the assets and resources—especially food, warmth, and space—controlled by other groups and communities that might be less adversely affected. Governments at all levels will be obliged to assume the role of mediator and to balance conflicting and competing demands. They will have to offer protection to both displaced populations and original inhabitants as populations shift to more desirable locations and settlements. Moreover, because the shifts were made necessary by nature, the problems of governance will often transcend national boundaries and require regional cooperation and integration on continent-wide scales.

Consequently, one major feature that will be unique about the future will be its proportions. For the past thousand years, the scope of human interaction and problems has been narrowing as more and more states have been created and greater differentiation has occurred. Religions, ethnic groups, and money have allowed people to remain isolated and to develop and improve their lives at vastly different rates. Just fifty years ago, the wealthy everywhere could be confident that by the conservation of their capital, the judicious application of the interest compounded on it, and the other forms of leverage it generated, they could guarantee the quality of their life styles more or less indefinitely and insulate themselves from the pressures and conflicts of the poor in their home countries and around the globe. Few people, rich or poor, think that way today.

The technology of tomorrow seems far more inclined toward and capable of scattering its power and benefits on a global scale than that which characterized the industrial revolution. Contact with the technology of the latter was limited to a few, usually those who worked in factories and on the manufacturing process. Far more than the consumers of their products or the managers who profited from their labor, the workers were normally the only people aware of the practical power of machines to produce materials better, faster, and cheaper. When workers eventually discovered that their skills in operating these technologies could translate into political power, they organized and were alternately powerful and repressed. In retrospect, labor unions and movements in nearly every country undergoing industrialization didn't really achieve a high degree of influence for very long. This was attributed in part to the fact that the workers did not own or control the technology, no matter how well they understood its operation. When the whistle blew and the workers left the shop floor, they left behind the benefits of the new technology. Only later as wages rose and the prices of manufactured goods began to decline in proportion to the workers' purchasing power did laborers actually see a relationship between what machines did for them at work and what they did for their families at home.

Today, farmers or workers can live in a world where the large-scale functions of machines at work can be downsized and replicated in their personal lives. Most technologies available to the chairman of IBM are available to the company's least-paid employee—as well as to the mechanic who services cars employees drive to work or the clerk in the grocery store who bags the food they consume. Although large amounts of capital will still be necessary to invent the applications of tomorrow, the machines and processes that are created will likely be reproduced to the point where the unit cost will be affordable to average people everywhere. And this distribution is bound to change people's expectations about their own lives and about the future they can provide for their children. As this occurs, the role and nature of government are also likely to change. People may find they need less assistance from government because they have access to more of the ideas and processes that will improve their lives. But above all, they will expect governments to facilitate equal access to the devices and procedures that improve the way we live as individuals and with each other. Governments have never before been held to this standard. But never have so many people been aware of the potential for technology to increase their productivity and security. Clearly, the technology of the future will be indispensable as well as accessible to everyone interested in freedom.

There is no telling what genius and creativity lie ahead as people are liberated by technology in the service of the idea of freedom. But consider the consequences. Currently, probably a quarter of the world's population cannot even read; half do not attend school for more than a few years. Yet these people's brain size and capacity for absorbing and applying knowledge are roughly the same as those of the reader of this book. Who can make a case that our future will be anything but brighter as these minds come on stream?

Notes

1. Reported in William J. Broad, "Breakthrough in Nuclear Fusion Offers Hope for Power of Future," *New York Times*, 11 November 1991, pp. 1, 11.

5

Prospects for Regional Integration and Conflict Resolution

The world of the twenty-first century will be far more integrated politically and economically than the current international system. This chapter suggests why this will happen, outlines the framework, and forecasts the implications of such integration. In many respects it is the hardest chapter to write for there is a prevailing sense that the European Community is the consummate example of efficient integration and that the other regions of the world are not capable of adapting such a comprehensive model given their traditions and needs. Even in the case of Europe, there are persistent doubts that the European Community can function effectively as a unit, especially if it grows larger or trade and currency issues become more contentious and politically significant now that the cold war is over. There are also doubts that the ethnic and nationalist rivalries—which have become more apparent with the collapse of communism—will allow for the creation of a single market, the establishment of a single currency, or the development of a common foreign and defense policy for an entire continent. As Danish voters demonstrated in the summer of 1992, there is even renewed debate over whether such objectives and features of integration are desirable.

There are also doubts that the process will exert appeal outside of Europe or that current and projected conflict, in other regions, will facilitate or promote integration. Hence the need to consider the close relationship between conflict and integration, especially at a time when the closer some belligerent parties move toward ending long-standing disputes, the more fringe and other extremist political forces resist. Clearly, integration must be based on a fusion of common interests and cannot evolve rapidly in the midst of disparate ethnic demands and simmering social hostilities.

The Role of Trade in Shaping International Relations

Like most of the sociopolitical forces discussed in this book, the trend toward regional integration in Europe—and interdependence among Europe, America, and Japan based on ever-freer trade—has been and apparently will remain uneven. Voters in some countries are reluctant to create a common currency, politicians in others disagree about security arrangements that could best handle post-cold war era conflicts and disorder, and selected agricultural interests are powerful enough to insist on retaining subsidies and protection that compromise the search for tariff reduction on a global basis. Such developments do not signal the end or the reversal of the process but the challenges involved in adapting the institutions, values, and processes of the EC to the new conditions of world political and economic life. Although how and when these challenges will be overcome is difficult to know in the short term, few Europeans today think they will be living in a less integrated region or world by the end of the century. The prospects for the next suggested here, moreover, indicate that an even greater premium will be placed on economic and political relationships based on the efficiencies, principles, and potential that the EC has come to represent.

Today, it seems the strongest advocates of the theory and practice of free trade are those countries that have benefited most from the management of the international system by military superpowers. Consequently, there is a tendency to argue that free trade is not the natural state of the world economy but is rather a condition imposed on it that requires considerable and continual effort by at least hegemons—if not superpowers—to enforce. Certainly the tensions over and questions about the fate of the General Agreement on Tariffs and Trade (GATT) or the Maastricht Treaty throughout 1991 and 1992 reinforce this perception.

But nothing is inherent in the concept of free trade that actually requires the type of international system and power balances described above. In fact, most Third World and many industrialized countries are finding they would rather maintain global access, with no barriers to the free flow of their goods and services, than to gain the protection of all native industries regardless of their level of efficiency. Such a system inevitably serves to develop more efficient and competitive domestic industries. In my forecast of the future, I think that this is likely to remain the case and that whatever the outcome of the current trade negotiations in the Uruguay Round of the GATT process, the long-term trend will be toward creating an international system that facilitates free trade. The protection required for some industries and social classes will be achieved inside the regional common markets that will also be erected—but even this degree of protection will not provide a significant damper to the flow of free trade over the long term because to maintain it would impair the ability of the market to compete effectively. The central point to remember here is that both regional integration and free trade will take place because such developments are in everyone's long-term interests and not because they were enforced as an adjunct of a system of managing international relationships that was dictated by either economic or military superpowers.

The Political Momentum Behind Integration

In reflecting on the European common market experience, my colleague, Berndt Von Staden, who is one of the senior statesmen of the movement that conceptualized and proposed the initiative, concluded that it had succeeded "beyond all expectation." This is a key observation to keep in mind for the future. Regional integration of the sort that has occurred in Europe has a tendency to proceed further—but not necessarily more rapidly—than its proponents envision. And the ingredients that will be required to inspire integration in other regions are now emerging on a global scale: the trend toward democratization; the free flow of ideas, people, and information; and the recognition—at micro as well as macro levels—that when a common interest is advanced, the individual is better and more efficiently served than when the economic interest of one constituency is pursued at the expense of others.

In many respects, it took Europe nearly a century to reach its present state. Two major wars and the presence of a Soviet threat were "required" to overcome most of the social, cultural, and political forces that divided the continent. The devastating results of these wars illustrated, to victor and vanquished alike, the need for and desirability of peaceful cooperation and integration. Today, there are abundant signs in Eastern Europe that these fundamental lessons have yet to be fully learned. In the case of the Yugoslavian civil war, the numerous press interviews with soldiers and victims on all sides, who continued to think warfare was necessary and the results were worthwhile, were sadly reminiscent of the past decades and the doctrines of divisive nationalism and militarism. Nevertheless, during the period of this civil war, as many people died on U.S. highways as perished in the combat that took place. So, one question we must keep in mind when contemplating the future is: Will war have to occur on a catastrophic scale—for example, in the Middle East or in Africa—in order to convince leaders in those regions to set aside ancient prejudices, as much of Europe has now done? I do not think so.

Although there is always a risk that leaders will fail to see the benefits of regional conflict resolution and integration, I think most will be unlikely to resist the process by the end of the 1990s. The world economy already points them in the direction of increasingly greater interdependence. In addition, in the process of seeking and demanding self-determination, the constant creation of more and smaller states will reinforce the need for integration and regional cooperation in order to provide economic viability and enhanced security for the nations being crafted out of the processes of self-determination now under way.

The scale of such states—coupled with the high degree of differentiation associated with the globalization of business—will further reinforce the need for and practice of interdependence and conflict resolution. Leaders must search for ways to preserve their country's uniqueness and at the same time, to maximize its participation in the international economy. This will mean that sooner rather than later, in order to survive states will have to relinquish some of the elements giving them independence of action. For some countries, this will mean giving up the dream and the dubious prestige associated with maintaining their own army in order to allocate limited resources more effectively to domestic social priorities. For most countries, the nature of global economic interdependence will thus provide powerful incentives to leaders to find their country's comparative advantage, improve on it, and enter into arrangements with other states to maintain and secure this advantage. In such a world, of course, free trade will be an essential prerequisite for the economic survival of all. For it is only in a global market environment, with no barriers to the exchange of goods and services, that nations are free to find what they can do best and what they are able to offer to others.

The most striking feature of the international economic system today is the degree to which it rewards regional integration and trade.[1] Regions tend to grow—and increase demands for goods and services—far faster than individual countries. The resources and capital people exchange within the region tend to be used very efficiently: More sellers can find more buyers, and individual nations are free to specialize in the production of profitable goods and services and to purchase what they do not have and what things they need from regional producers. In the past, many nations were forced to diversify production or to tap natural resources in order to ensure economic independence and national security. As the process evolves and more goods and services are exchanged, more income is created to allow people to improve their lives and develop tastes for additional goods and services produced outside the region. As this occurs, the region attracts extra-regional investment, and this creates jobs and even more income.

The bottom line is that through regional integration—or at least through the creation of common market arrangements—the majority of the people will benefit and trade will increase as more buyers begin to search for more sellers and, due to population growth, there are more and more customers, even for those commodities now in surplus. Regionalization also promotes democratization and political stability. It tends to create an atmosphere and an impetus for countries to respect basic human rights across all types of systems; it also allows goods, capital, and people to move freely and puts subtle economic and social pressure on individual countries to reduce illegal or unscheduled political actions and changes that jeopardize the continued attraction of extra-regional resources and direct investment. Never in history has a regional market succeeded by closing itself off to the rest of the world.

Present Obstacles

Of course, numerous past attempts at regional integration have not been successful. However, the most encouraging lesson derived from these failures is that virtually every study points to the lack of political will on the part of those who had the chance to participate in these attempts and not to the impracticability of such arrangements for enhancing economic growth and trade. No one has really demonstrated that integration makes poor economic sense, only that many leaders thus far have lacked the vision and courage to surmount the initial obstacles to its creation. Consequently, I think it is at least possible to foresee a period in which the appeal of political incentives for integration will grow at both the mass and elite levels and that this will overcome the resistance that has derailed past efforts.

Yet, many obstacles to free trade and regional integration currently remain. But these obstacles result from a temporary state of world order, as it moves to another system and level of order, rather than from any inherent or long-term tendency to counteract the phenomenon. The implication of this statement is that as the shape of the post-cold war world comes into clearer view, so also will the benefits of the kind of integration described above. Eventually, in virtually every region, the incentive will exist to create common markets and more coordinated foreign policies. Nations will accept interdependence to a much larger degree in the quest for trade and prosperity than they currently have in this century in the quest for military security.

The nature and definition of new world orders very much preoccupy our thoughts these days for many of us have never lived at a time when the international order—and the balance of power among the states within it—was so unclear and transitory. We also have very little in the way of analogous historical experience and points of reference. Bipolar systems are also fairly rare. The only contemporary example of such a system is the recently ended U.S.-Soviet model, which evolved after World War II. Traditionally, the international system has not dissolved into a period of unipolar dominance, even following a major world war—when the tendency has been for new powers to rise and a system of multipolarity to evolve immediately in order to fill the void of vanquished powers. In the past, when this change occurred we were able to identify the top powers by their possession of great military and economic strength.

Today, the international system is composed of countries that are strong economically but not militarily (e.g., Germany, Japan, and the Asian Tigers) and those that still possess tremendous military capabilities but find it unrealistic to project power in this way (e.g., the United States and Russia). A large range of countries in between these extremes (e.g., Indonesia, South Africa, Egypt, and Brazil) are also significant and pivotal players in the future due to their size, geography, and active involvement in world affairs. Clearly, all of these countries have different views of the emerging world order, the role they should play in it, and the forces and principles to which it should respond. All will look partly to their own historical experiences for clues as to how they should behave and what new policies they should advocate. But, as I have suggested, such historical experience will provide little guidance for the future because we need to begin thinking that in the multiplicity and interdependence of the powers in it, the world that is emerging is unique from any of the past ages. The world of the future has a new resource and set of relationships to build on, especially as the phenomenon of regional integration unfolds.

Integration will not be a panacea. It will not be without pain and cost to those workers and enterprises that provide functions and skills that may become expendable as they find themselves to be inefficient or nonessential. This is why it is vital to maintain a long-term view. The world will not develop into a collection of common markets overnight—as is evident in the case of Europe, which has been arguing over the nature, shape, and scope of the metamorphosis of the community since its inception. But over time, the benefits of integration have consistently proved more valuable than the apparent alternatives. So, it is reasonable to expect that at some point in the 1990s, the European Community will make even more rapid progress toward creating a United States of Europe than the most extreme optimists would forecast today. Who else will follow?

Will the countries that emerge by the mid to late 1990s out of the breakup of the Soviet Union or the resolution of the Arab-Israeli-Palestinian conflict follow the same course? Can Africans also look forward to economic communities when their current development prospects are so bleak and all previous efforts to form such entities foundered and then failed as national ambitions and ethnic antipathies surfaced to erode what progress had been made? Will leaders in the Middle East be able to set aside the prejudices of thousands of years to practice toleration because they want freer trade?

I think the answers to these questions are decidedly affirmative. The experience of the 1980s confirmed and reinforced the theory that economic growth and development cannot be achieved in isolation by individual nations. It did this because our world was already in the process of a fundamental transformation. The world economy is now too sensitive and demanding to allow countries to make much progress behind trade barriers or aggrandizing policies that are premised on the assumption that one country's gain can only be achieved by another's loss. Increasingly, leaders will be searching for more comprehensive non-zero-sum gains through economic growth. This endeavor will prove politically and culturally popular.

Trade brings a higher and richer quality of life. We should not lose sight of the fact that this has been a universal certainty ever since the Neolithic era, when humans began to abandon their caves and the hunting-and-gathering style of life and settle into villages. Approximately ten thousand years ago, our ancestors began to think about exchanging what they had for what they wanted. Even though this barter system was no doubt initially difficult for some to accept, when it was discovered that the bounty of some hunters was more valuable than that of others who were less skilled at finding game, over time each person in this primitive society adapted to activities and crafts that would best enable him or her to secure what was wanted. This realization / transformation was accelerated by the stunning growth of urban life, where goods and services could be readily exchanged. In fact, by the year 7000 B.C., around ten cities in the ancient world probably had populations greater than one hundred thousand.

The modern sequel to this transformation—and the contribution trade and systems of interdependence can make to assuring that it occurs peacefully—is illustrated by the state of Europe after World War II. Although the continent was devastated economically, the sources of ethnic, religious, ideological, and national rivalries and conflicts were left largely intact. Indeed, in 1945, Europe seemed to be an unlikely candidate for regional integration, and the notions of those who favored such a development appeared visionary at best and seemed illusory to most. Few other continents had experienced such a history of warfare and division. Nowhere else had there been so many wars or attempts at genocide.

Yet today, we are observing a profound change in Europe due to the power of the idea of integration. Although many European writers have captured the essence of what transpired for the purposes of this book, I was struck most by the non-European perceptions of the European experiment. This knowledge gives us insight into the global appeal of the European integration concept and the future chances for its replication. In this context, I was very impressed by the intercultural character of a recent statement by Sony chairman Akio Morita in reflecting on the meaning of European integration for the future of U.S.-Japanese relations. "It is widely known that Europe . . . comprises numerous nations and embraces a large variety of languages and cultures. Throughout its history Europe has seen many changes in national boundaries and spheres of influence among individual states. European nations have often been far from congenial with one another. The integration of the European Community is, thus, a trial of different nations' ability to cooperate economically for the greater good, by limiting individual sovereign rights and national interests. "[2]

The Future Appeal of Integration

Regional integration can have the same positive effects and consequences on a worldwide scale. The concept should appeal to people and their emerging leaders in many regions, even though it will inevitably require that nations relinquish some degree of sovereignty and redefine national interests to encompass interdependence. Consider, for example, the potential represented by the fifteen members of the newly formed Asia Pacific Economic Cooperation organization. This effort to create a regional dialogue, focusing on projects and institutions that would promote cooperation and economic growth, affects the future prosperity of 40 percent of the world's present population; by the year 2000, this proportion will have grown to well over 50 percent. Should a common market ultimately be established for this region, its members could account for more than half of the world's trade by the first quarter of the twenty-first century. Presumably, there will be tensions in the evolutionary process, and all leaders and systems will not acclimate to the new demands and circumstances at the same time or rate. However, the experience of Europe will serve as a model and a guide for mechanisms, processes of conflict resolution, pitfalls, and the scope of benefits that integration can be expected to provide for all.

As the structure of European integration becomes more refined and prosperity becomes more widely shared within it, leaders in other regions will come under increasing pressure to secure similar advantages. Powerful nations will be tempted to assemble their own regional groups in order to maintain their former levels of economic growth and power. If the United States aligns with Canada, Mexico, or other Latin American nations and Japan joins with Korea, Hong Kong, Singapore, or other Asian partners in regional associations, the international system will be characterized not by a balance of power (there will be no military or security-related need for one) but by the interaction and interdependence of entire regions, rich and poor.

Inevitably, regional powers will replace national powers in the new international system. By the end of the 1990s, the model of European prosperity will inspire a flood of attempts to create common markets. Consequently, regional groups will materialize in the Pacific, the Middle East, South Asia, and Africa. By the years 2010 to 2025, a multitude of regional common markets may well be thriving.

This forecast is not surprising; what is surprising is the considerable activity toward these ends that is already under way. Numerous influential regional and subregional organizations have been created in the past decade. They currently exist on every continent, and more are under consideration. Of course, some of these organizations will be impotent, and some will fragment and disappear. However, the points I am emphasizing are that the potential exists, the benefits are being explored, and the process is well under way.

■ PROSPECTS FOR REGIONAL INTEGRATION: DATELINE AFRICA
—Sandra Clemens McMahon

At the start of the 1990s, the building of regional organizations was accelerated by visions of new frontiers and opportunities; by the year 2000, it may be driven by a basic instinct for survival. An increasing number of leaders on the African continent are acutely aware of this trend. When member states of the Organization for African Unity (OAU) adopted the Abuja Treaty in June 1991, which called for establishing a Pan-Africa Economic Community (PAEC) by the year 2025, they were responding to the challenges posed by the creation and expansion of regional trading blocs in other areas of the globe. They were also struggling to achieve economic survival.

Today, a combination of several factors threatens to isolate Africa from world markets; these include the success of the U.S.-Canada Free Trade Agreement and the recent incorporation of Mexico into the partnership, the establishment of the Australia-New Zealand Free Trade Area, the creation of a new economic bloc in Asia and the Far East, the progress toward a limited State of Europe, and even the appearance of the newly formed Black Sea economic grouping composed of eleven Balkan and former Soviet nations. Suddenly, the pressure to achieve regional economic integration has become more intense in order to compete with existing regional organizations, as well as to combat Africa's seemingly chronic economic underdevelopment and to reverse the continent's growing marginalization in world affairs.

Africa is a large continent, but it is fragmented into numerous small markets. Currently, more than two hundred regional organizations are functioning in Africa. Many of them are small, specialized, and ineffective. In fact, trade within African borders has hardly grown in the past twenty years and accounts for only 5 percent of all African trade. Smuggling also occurs on a large scale. The revitalization of African economic growth will demand an increase in production levels and, subsequently, the development of both African and world markets. Internal trade is at the core of African economic growth because European and North American trading blocs can increasingly limit the flow of African exports to their regions. However, the divisive political environment in Africa, fueled by cold war fears and rivalries and myriad competing subregional organizations, has encouraged little progress toward the stimulation of continental trade. In order to finance the path to economic recovery and successful integration, African leaders are now aware that cooperation and economic progress, such as the agreement to create a PAEC, are vital.

As the primary continental grouping, the OAU has shown renewed leadership and inspired cohesion by ushering in the Abuja Treaty and promoting the concept of a Pan-African Economic Community. Unfortunately, the larger scope of OAU actions is limited by factors such as the political nature of the organization, its complex and bureaucratic structure, the unwieldy number of members (fifty-one at last count), and the limited supply of institutional resources. Because the heads of state act as representatives of their nations within the OAU structure, primal, political instincts of self-preservation often prevail in the policymaking process. Within this context, regional decisions may be framed primarily to perpetuate existing governments rather than to promote long-term continental development, and overall regional objectives may be overlooked.

In view of these institutional limitations and in response to the magnitude and complexity of the task ahead for Africa, hybrid organizations that unite public and private interests have evolved to fill a gap in the process of policy coordination and implementation. One such example, the Global Coalition for Africa (GCA), was launched in 1991 as an informal, high-level political forum to help create a more effective development partnership between Africa and the international community. The proposal spawning the GCA was endorsed by the African heads of state meeting in July 1991. The GCA has three co-chairmen: Sir Ketumile Masire, president of Botswana; Jan P. Pronk, minister of Development Cooperation of the Netherlands; and Robert S. McNamara, former president of the World Bank. The participants are African decisionmakers—including economic ministers and heads of state—as well as representatives of major regional and international organizations, bilateral donor nations, and other development partners in Africa.

The GCA functions as a catalyst to energize and coordinate existing resources in order to mobilize international support for African progress. It provides an umbrella framework to support new and ongoing initiatives and a forum where decisionmakers from Africa and the international community can discuss issues, reach consensus on long-term development issues and programs of actions, and then return to their organizations to implement the plans. Promoting regional economic integration and cooperation is a priority of the coalition. One immediate goal of the GCA is to help African countries in their execution of the Abuja agreement and to monitor their progress. In order to achieve this goal, according to documents issued in 1991 and 1992 by the Global Coalition for Africa in Washington, D.C., the GCA secretariat is working closely with the EC and African institutions to assure that regional integration is demand-driven and to strengthen African institutional capacity to design and manage programs.

Another such hybrid, nongovernmental organization, the African Leadership Forum (ALF), recently took the initiative to propose that Africa establish its own version of the "Helsinki" process and launch a Conference on Peace, Security, Stability, Development, and Cooperation in Africa (CSSDCA). This plan for regional cooperation emanated from the Kampala Forum, which was attended by five hundred current and former African heads of state as well as private and institutional representatives. The resulting Kampala Document outlines a long-term framework for continental development and cooperation. As a result, the 1991 OAU summit of African Heads of State and Government acknowledged for the first time that "there is a link between security, stability, development, and cooperation in Africa," and leaders at the OAU summit recognized that the lack of security and stability in many African countries has impaired their capacity to achieve a sufficient level of cooperation within and integration of the continent. The Kampala Document also calls for fundamental changes with respect to governance in Africa and identifies democratization as a prerequisite for peace and progress in African development and regional organization. According to the document, which was published by the ALF in 1991, the African Leadership Forum chairman, General Olusegun Obasanjo, former head of state of Nigeria, observed that the concepts of the Kampala proposal were popular among an overwhelming majority of African nations in attendance at the OAU summit, and he is encouraged by the positive initial response to the CSSDCA and is optimistic about the future of the initiative.

In short, African development has a new orientation. The future of African regional organization and integration is being shaped by international as well as regional, and private as well as public actors. Cooperative ventures on a global scale—uniting African continental, regional, and subregional organizations, international institutions, representatives of other nations, and private actors in a concerted effort to achieve African regional cooperation— present a unique solution to a complex problem. In the end, they may help African countries to derive greater benefits from the emerging international order and to shed the chronic condition of economic underdevelopment.

> —Compiled from S.K.B. Asanter, "New Hope for Africa," *Development and Cooperation*, No. 4 (Frankfurt am Main: German Foundation for International Development, 1992), p. 20; Africa Leadership Forum, *The Kampala Document*, New York, 1991; and Global Coalition for Africa, reports and press releases, 1991.

■

What makes me think such a system and network of common markets will enhance free trade rather than act as powerful barriers to it? Certainly, the image and fear of a fortress Europe have been frequently invoked as the community moves ever closer to full integration. But a common market will not succeed by preventing trade or by closing itself off to the rest of the world. It just trades differently as a unit than it would if individual countries were involved in the transactions. Hence, this principle explains the striking phenomenon that the EC's trade with the rest of the world has grown faster and is in fact greater (as a portion of most countries' gross domestic product) than trade within the community. The experience suggests that the erection of the European Community has facilitated, rather than restricted, trade with other regions.

Now clearly, there may be some limits to how many regional markets in the future can accomplish this same level and diversity of growth in economic and social activities. Some, when they come into being, will not yet have the product and service mixes that enable them to export effectively outside their circle. Yet, there should be no technical limits to growth because each region will have vast internal markets that presumably will be better served, and each will have more rapid population growth than the established common markets of the 1990s (e.g., Europe, U.S.-Canada-Mexico). This increase in both the labor and consumer force will most likely prove to be beneficial. Indeed, I foresee a period in which the industrialized countries' exports to the Third World may actually decline on a per capita basis as internal markets there satisfy the demand for food, manufactured goods, and services far more efficiently. For what the advanced countries may have unwittingly developed by the end of this century are systems of management and production that in fact can function just as well in Third World settings and will be transplanted there by the tendency toward globalism in corporate enterprise. Suddenly, it will cease to matter to IBM, Philips, or Hitachi not only where product lines are sourced but also where they are manufactured; freedom, technology, education, and communications will make it much more possible to locate plants anywhere, especially those locales characterized by large and rapidly growing populations, and then customize the product for the tastes and requirements of local as well as global consumers.

Challenges for the United States

What are the implications of the developments forecast above for the United States? One question in particular springs to mind in regard to American influence in regional European politics through the North Atlantic Treaty Organization (NATO)—namely, will it continue? The NATO military alliance has traditionally assured the United States a voice in European policies, without its having to suffer through the formal application process for membership in the common market. There is considerable apprehension over the implications of decoupling U.S. and European defense establishments and doctrines—or the process by which it will be achieved—but few expect that by the year 2000, one-third of the U.S. defense budget will continue to be spent for the defense of Europe.

It will be a long good-bye. Events and trends in the former Soviet Union are far from encouraging or even clear. It will be at least 1995 before policy planners in the U.S. Department of Defense are certain that the post-Soviet threat has been eliminated (and all its nuclear weapons have been either dismantled or placed in safe hands) and for European leaders to create a consensus for the establishment of region-wide armies and alliance structures that do not require a primus inter pares to mediate between conflicting claims to leadership and to restrain tendencies to take unilateral action in future crises. It is vital that these leaders also become more comfortable with political cooperation—the still all-too-rare analog to economic integration—and that they see political cooperation register some genuine success in containing and resolving regional conflicts.

It need not be a traumatic good-bye. And this is the real challenge in the management of the U.S.-European defense alliance system, which has served us so well for so long. A method must be found to conceptualize the evolution of this relationship so the eventual withdrawal of U.S. forces and money will not be perceived as hasty, undesirable, or a symbol of the decline of American power and interest on either side of the Atlantic. This anxiety is always present in the minds of European leaders because the traditional U.S. tendency has been to end its wars by retreating into isolationism. However, the global situation has changed so substantially in the past decade that isolationism is no longer a viable alternative for any nation, even one that turns sharply inward to focus on domestic problems.

The impact elsewhere of the trend toward regional integration is not yet fully apparent. Although much international attention has already been focused on the significance of the implementation of the Single European Act, leaders within the EC are expanding their horizons by considering a political union that could incorporate the democratizing countries of Eastern Europe as well as the republics of the Commonwealth of Independent States.[3] Meanwhile, regional economic and political organizations are being created or significantly strengthened in every part of the globe. As the role and power projection capabilities of the superpowers have declined in the face of their internal problems, such initiatives and organizations have enhanced the influence of second-order powers in both regional and world politics. Consider, for example, the fact that over the past several years major initiatives to resolve regional conflicts have already come from leaders of such countries as Costa Rica, Egypt, India, and Indonesia, as well as from the United States and the U.S.S.R. In view of the increasing numbers and influence of regional organizations, more is likely to be heard from Third World representatives of these regional groups in regard to the threats to regional and global security— and how to reduce them—as well as about ways to solve transnational issues.[4]

Thus, there is also a risk that the trend toward regionalism and economic and political integration will not be a welcome one from a U.S. perspective. Despite the public rhetoric about U.S. support for a unified Germany and a United States of Europe and, more important, for the so-called Pacific century that is to follow, most Americans today are neither conceptually nor strategically prepared for these developments. The persistence of the U.S. budget and trade deficits, for example, may make us less able to compete in a more economically integrated world or to do so without the benefit of protectionism. Other projected developments in world politics could lead to the estrangement of the United States from some of its major relationships. For example, the need to finance democratization in the republics of the former

Soviet Union but our reluctance to do so could result in the development of a very close relationship between Japan and the Commonwealth of Independent States, on the one hand,[5] and in Western and Eastern Europe being more able to act in concert than the members of the NATO alliance, on the other.

The United States is also likely to find that it is increasingly difficult to exert influence on regional issues and problems. Aid budget constraints will certainly limit U.S. influence in black Africa, where many leaders resent the very high priority that is placed on helping Eastern European countries that have recently renounced communism. In comparison, the states in the Third World have been struggling for decades to achieve democratization and develop capitalist systems. Foreign policy constraints are also apparent in the Middle East. In this region, two decades of vacillation over the question of the existence and terms of a Palestinian homeland (and on whose territory)—coupled with political uncertainty in Washington over how long the consensus between the executive and the legislative branches and among U.S. allies abroad will endure—have restricted the American capability to break out of the set of forces and dynamics causing periodic crises. Finally, in Central and South America, U.S. prestige and influence could be weakened by insensitivity toward the economic and social effects of tightening immigration policies and our perceived failure to punish politicians and other white-collar criminals who use drugs.[6] Furthermore, in all regions our ability to promote democratization will decline if the United States continues to rely on covert action operations as a means of promoting political change. In many instances, covert actions invade a nation's sovereignty and right to self-determination if they are employed as a means of combatting home-grown revolutions.

The U.S. foreign policy establishment, thus, is facing the future with uncertainty about how it will evolve and lack of consensus over what our role can and ought to be. This particular conjunction of doubts over policy and of our ability to implement it once it has been selected is a novel dilemma confronting Washington policymakers. How we respond to this situation—and especially how we project and share our views about the meaning of the new international order—will be critical to the future global prestige and prosperity of the United States. From now on, in order to maintain our democratic image and competitive status, the United States may well have to avoid the impulse to impose its values and will on nations or regions that respect its principles and power but that also possess the resources to check its actions and that have increasingly strong and independent views of why the international order is changing and what its shape should be in the twenty-first century. Conflict resolution in the next century, therefore, is likely to be a much more widely shared responsibility, which should be a very positive development for the United States.

In this century, we have had to take the lead—albeit reluctantly—and our efforts have been greatly complicated by the rise of fascism and later communism. Hence, we developed the tendency to take on allies and causes with needs and priorities very dissimilar to our own and to become involved in limited wars we seemingly could not win and ultimately believed should not have been fought. In the period ahead, although America's fate will be even more closely tied to the state of the world, the dynamics of the international system itself will reinforce the need to end the present conflicts and will prevent or contain others before they necessitate superpower intervention.

Ironically, such a system is likely to be more successful than the one we helped to construct after World War II because the impetus for conflict resolution will come from those with a greater and more immediate stake in solutions—and in assuring that economic life and social intercourse continue without strain—than distant North American or European powers. This means future conflicts will not escalate to the point where they are menacing enough to capture our attention or directly threaten our security before those most immediately affected will take action. It also means we will not have to maintain a comprehensive global defense posture and capability to project our power but rather only have the good diplomatic sense and patience to use U.N. mechanisms like the Security Council and the Military Staff Commission to encourage a multinational force to step in when peacemaking is required.

This vision of the future will probably not materialize before the end of the present century, and in any case, our defense establishment may be very slow to recognize the signs that it is coming. The world today contains too many sources of tensions—old as well as new—to allow planners to relax or to assume that the problems that have prompted our use of force in the past are going to disappear any time soon. For the moment, they are right. But the key elements to watch are the trends sketched in this chapter, most especially those stimulating greater regional integration. If the source of most interstate warfare in history has been the enmity of one neighbor for another, it is their growing interdependence now that could altogether eliminate international conflict in the future.

Notes

1. The case for this is made by Robert Z. Lawrence, "Emerging Regional Arrangements: Building Blocks or Stumbling Blocks?" in Richard O'Brien, ed., *Finance and the International Economy 5: The Amex Bank Review Prize Essays*, New York: Oxford University Press, 1991.

2. *Japan Update* (Tokyo: Keizai Koho Center, November 1991), p. 3.

3. See, for example, the forecast by German chancellor Helmut Kohl contained in his commencement address at Harvard University, reprinted in *Harvard Alumni Gazette* (June 1990), pp. 24 and 32, and the types of questions that were to be addressed

Prospects for Regional Integration

at the EC's Conference on Political Union in December 1990, as reported in "European Council Presidency Conclusions," *European Community News*, No. 26 (27 June 1990).

4. Yezid Sayigh, *Confronting the 1990s: Security in the Developing Countries*, Adelphi Paper No. 251 (London: Summer 1990).

5. For a review of Soviet thinking on this subject, see Scott Atkinson, "The USSR and the Pacific Century," *Asian Survey*, 30 (July 1990), pp. 629-645.

6. See James Brooke, "Near-Acquittal of Barry Outraging Colombians," *New York Times*, 27 August 1990, p. A6.

6

The Obsolescence of War

Perhaps the most exciting aspect of the future is that the trends discussed in this book will act as catalysts to accelerate the growing obsolescence of interstate warfare in international affairs. In many cases, societal change is still associated with conflict and turmoil. For instance, the breakup of the former Soviet Union and of the Communist states of Eastern Europe did not give birth to new countries without some considerable degree of violence. However, the number and intensity of wars have been steadily decreasing. In 1986, the U.N. Year of Peace, there were more than twenty-five ongoing interstate wars. By the middle of 1992, no interstate wars were being fought, and the level of violence associated with internal conflicts was declining in many cases. As the accompanying box shows, moreover, in virtually every one of these conflicts, a robust peacekeeping or peacemaking effort is under way or has recently ended.

■ **U.N. PEACEKEEPING EFFORTS**

Current Operations

El Salvador	ONUSAL—U.N. observer force	Since 7/1991
Yugoslavia	UNPROFOR—U.N. protection force	Since 3/1992
Cyprus	UNFICYP—U.N. force	Since 1964
India/Pakistan	UNMOGIP—U.N. observer group	Since 1948
Cambodia	UNAMIC—U.N. advance mission	Since 10/1991
	UNTAC—U.N. transitional authority	Since 3/1992
Iraq/Kuwait	UNIKOM—U.N. observation mission	Since 4/1991
Lebanon	UNIFIL—U.N. interim force	Since 1978
Golan Heights	UNDOF—U.N. disengagement observer force	Since 1974
Angola	UNAVEM II—New U.N. verification mission	Since 6/1991
Western Sahara	MINURSO—U.N. mission for the referendum	Since 9/1991
Somalia	UNOSOM—U.N. operation	Since 4/1992

Recent Operations

Central America	ONUCA—U.N. observer group	11/1989 to 1/1992
Iran/Iraq	UNIIMOG—U.N. military observer group	8/1988 to 2/1991
Namibia	UNTAG—U.N. transition assistance group	4/1989 to 3/1990
Angola	UNAVEM—U.N. verification mission	12/1988 to 5/1992
Afghanistan/		
Pakistan	UNGOMAP—U.N. good offices mission	4/1988 to 3/1990

■

Clearly, more activity lies ahead for the United Nations. But I foresee it as a prelude to ending conflicts of most types because there will be less war in the twenty-first century. Why?

The End of All That?

When Operation Desert Storm ended, President Bush declared both the advent of a new world order and the end of the Vietnam syndrome. Neither is fully true, of course, but the reference to Vietnam especially reminds us that we have been deeply and not altogether successfully involved in a considerable number of wars and conflicts in this century.

The end of the Vietnam War is a good place to start thinking about how wars can lead to peace. In 1975, Asia was certainly not at peace and prospects were far from bright for the evolution of the region in ways the United States would have wanted if the outcome in Vietnam had been different. With the exception of Japan, the countries of the region were governed by well-entrenched dictatorships that seemed invulnerable to pressures to expand political participation or respect human rights. The extent to which China would renew support for insurgencies in Southeast Asia—many of which were started with Beijing's help—was far from clear, as was the overall thrust of China's foreign policy as it began to emerge from a decade of isolation caused by the failed cultural revolution. Sino-Soviet hostilities had not lessened, and the North Vietnamese victory led to brutal repression against the indigenous Chinese in Vietnam that, as it turned out, created a casus belli for a war between these two countries in 1978.

So, the order we had hoped might accompany a *Pax Americana* in Asia after Vietnam was instead replaced by disorder. Between 1975 and 1980, the region was marked by political upheaval, two wars (China versus Vietnam and the conflict over Cambodia/Kampuchea), growing trade tensions with the United States, student rebellions in Korea and Thailand, and the restriction of the freedom of the press in a number of countries.

Immobilized by the fall of Saigon and then paralyzed by the Watergate scandal, Washington responded to very few of these events creatively and was almost always on the wrong side. Here enters the Vietnam syndrome. It refers to many things: the way we got involved in the region's conflicts with little regard to their internal causes or dynamics, the faulty appraisals of the strength and legitimacy of the forces with which we allied, and the inability to generate domestic support for such involvement so it could last as long as might be required. In the years since 1975, when the last chopper left the rooftop of the U.S. Embassy in Saigon, consequently, Washington intervened in a number of conflicts in reaction to Soviet and Cuban adventurism, found itself supporting the most repressive dictators, and was so concerned that public support for such involvement would rapidly erode if the extent of the intervention were to become common knowledge that it planned and conducted many of these operations as covert actions.

Did all this change with the outcome of Desert Storm? The U.S. public will remain very reluctant to use force in international affairs, especially at a time when our main "enemy" has been neutralized and dismembered. As long as the Commonwealth of Independent States, which succeeded the Soviet Union, shows no propensity to use force in global matters, the United States will not be compelled to intervene in most conflicts that will arise. We will remain, consequently, hesitant to use force and uncertain about our ability to prevail.

Moreover, the war to liberate Kuwait was too short and easy to prove conclusively that the failures and insecurities that plagued us in the case of Vietnam are now far behind us. Our forces met very little resistance and none as clever as the strategies orchestrated by our adversary in Indochina. The ground attack was the first in this century that was undertaken by an army that possessed complete control of the air. The majority of Americans cheered on their superior military team. They applauded as the deployment of technologically advanced weapons was successful to a surprising and unprecedented extent. Although most of the new weapons had not been tested in combat, the development of sophisticated computer modeling techniques and intensive military training exercises has made it possible to test and perfect weapons and procedures in advance of actual combat. Because the tempo of the war was speedy and the results were victorious, public and international support never had the chance to dwindle.

In one sense, our war with Iraq is not over. Although Iraq suffered a temporary setback, Operation Desert Storm did not eliminate Saddam Hussein and his regime or destroy all of his production facilities for weapons of mass destruction. The future of Kuwait in political terms, moreover, is far from clear. Although the military offensive of the coalition forces served to restore the former Kuwaiti political structure and to reinstate the deposed leadership, the victors have witnessed the outcome with mixed emotions.

Unfortunately, the past system of government in Kuwait was questionable by
U.S. standards, and the present system has not been significantly reformed or
democratized. Operation Desert Storm did little to improve the leadership on
the Arabian peninsula or to guarantee the commitment of the royal families to
issues of democratization and human rights. Consequently, there is still a
legitimate debate over what we actually gained through the use of force in Iraq.
Many people question whether the basic political, human rights, and security
issues that were at stake and still remain so can be solved by fighting and even
winning another war.

Although we emerged as the victors in the war against Iraq, we have also
discovered that triumph in war does not necessarily lead to the realization of
regional security goals. In the case of Iraq, although we achieved our
limited aims of liberating Kuwait, securing the flow of oil, defending Saudi
Arabia, and halting the development of nuclear weapons, the larger issue of
containing or deposing a despotic and dangerous ruler remains to be solved.

Furthermore, the costs of war now make us question its prudence. Was too
much force used? As technology affords global visibility and instant accessibility
to battles and casualty statistics, the stages of war become a more personal
experience, and the public tends to feel less comfortable with the results of each
battle. The casualties inflicted on the civilian population of Iraq will probably
never be accurately known in human, cultural, and development terms.
Unfortunately, unlike the case following any other war we fought and thought
we would win, we have not approached the vanquished—nor are we likely to
do so—with a plan for reconstruction contingent on pledges to assure that the
country would henceforth eschew the use of force in global relations and move
toward complete integration into an international system based on the rule of
law. What did we gain?

As a result of the Gulf war, what assurances for future accord have we
solicited from the governments of Kuwait and Saudi Arabia? Can we be certain
that they will actively seek to eliminate the dangerous social conditions and
ideological attitudes that have given dictators like Saddam Hussein reasons to
hope that naked aggression can be emotionally and politically justified by a
pan-Arab commitment to the destruction of Israel, which is portrayed as the
eternal, villainous enemy? How confident can we be that these governments
will now take steps to provide adequately for their own defense—or again
allow non-Arab forces into their territory for the purpose of deterring
aggression? Hardly any answers to such questions have been provided.

It is apparent that the U.S. political structure is still a source of domestic
discord during wartime. In Vietnam, the U.S. government constantly misled
itself, the Congress, and the public. In the aftermath of Desert Storm, there was
no indication that the U.S. foreign policy decisionmaking system, which
allowed confusing economic supports and faulty diplomatic signals to mislead
Saddam Hussein into assuming we would regard his invasion of Kuwait as an

"Arab-Arab affair," would be changed. Official actions continue to be followed by gaps and unanswered questions. The public is still confused about the actual context of the message our envoy relayed to the Iraqi leader when a distinct warning was alleged to have been given. We do not know—much less understand—how we could have ignored the obvious buildup of Iraqi forces along the border with Kuwait for such a long period in June and July 1990. In addition, we have no clear explanation from the Pentagon and the Central Intelligence Agency as to why they underestimated the progress of the Iraqi nuclear weapons development program.

In short, Desert Storm was not a war to end all wars or a model of what to do in the future. It was a war of limited objectives and very limited results. As such, it did not succeed in eliminating myriad regional threats or leaders with intentions and the capabilities to make war in the future. However, the denouement of the conflict did indicate a key lesson for our changing world order: Such wars, whether in pursuit of limited or expansive objectives, cannot guarantee a lasting peace. The questions for the longer term are, how many more wars lie ahead, and will the trend toward the use of force in international affairs increase or decrease?

Not every war to be fought in the 1990s will be about the struggle to create a new world order, nor will each be resolved in the name of its principles. Some conflicts, like that over the breakup of Yugoslavia, will be initiated and ended along the unfortunate lines of past hatreds and pathologies. Therefore, these wars may appear to reward aggression and demonstrate the selective application of the principles invoked in Operations Desert Shield and Desert Storm. But especially if the settlement of the civil war in Yugoslavia favors those who renounced mediation and thwarted U.N. peacekeepers, the experience will have taught the international community and the EC in particular what must be done to prevent and deter violence and armed intervention in such conflicts at the outset of any process by which new nations come into being. For in the case of both Kuwait and Yugoslavia, the critical and far more cost-effective stage for application of the principles of a new world order would have been during the period when those intending to violate these principles were making their plans and developing the capabilities to strike.

As a result of lessons derived from these current and anticipated conflicts, future attention to the intelligence information and policy coordination needed prior to the outbreak of hostilities will increase. This new focus will enhance the role of the United Nations, as well as the regional economic and political unions, as peacemakers in situations where timely disclosure, intervention to prevent further military buildups, and arrangements for negotiation could substantially reduce the likelihood that any party would judge war to be in its best interest or the only remaining option.

The Declining Appeal of Force

Another way to view what lies ahead in terms of the possibility of making war obsolete is to explore the conditions affecting how a leader of tomorrow will weigh the use of force in international affairs.

As a result of the forces and trends discussed in this book, a would-be aggressor will be aware that to conduct a war—or even threaten credibly to do so—will take enormous resources and a prolonged commitment to the course of action, once it is selected. Such aggressors will be dependent on a range of actors (i.e., generals and lesser military officials) who may be reluctant to risk their lives and careers, or who simply may not be motivated to fight for the cause identified. The buildup to and actual use of force will be difficult, if not impossible, to conceal. Consequently, little may be possible in the way of surprise due to the intrusiveness of media communications and national technical means of monitoring military maneuvers. Furthermore, the outcome of the conflict cannot be certain; indeed, every war in the second half of the twentieth century has ended along lines far different from those the people who started it had envisioned and planned. For the duration of the period or threat of war, trade will be ruptured and other economic relationships will be disturbed that increasingly are equally as relevant to a country's security as the relationships its leaders are able to maintain because of the military might they possess or are willing to exercise.

Under these circumstances, and given such prospects as those discussed above, it seems to me that the strategic equation is more complicated when it relates to the use of force and that the case for the utility of war is less and less compelling in an integrated, interdependent world order. To a great extent, moreover, the causes of war will also have diminished given the encouraging developments that lie ahead in the rule of international law and the growth of global and regional regimes to control the flow of arms and resolve local disputes.

The principal argument against these prospects is human nature. Apparently, humans do not renounce the use of force and violence easily, and some believe it is in our nature both to kill others and to find systems of values that justify our doing so in the name of the state. But most wars did not start because Cain slew Abel; the aggressors concluded there were sufficient political and economic reasons for fighting. The point I am making in this book about the most likely course for the future is that the changes now under way in the world order and those that lie ahead could end the necessity for most types of war.

I imagine a future where the propensity to use force is very low and the frequency of conflict is reduced to the greatest extent in history. I do not imagine this occurring or even coming into view within the next three to five years, but certainly by the end of the first quarter of the twenty-first century.

Little explanation is required to rationalize the years of residual conflict that lie ahead. Saddam Hussein is not the last of the autocrats who possess significant armies; the end of the cold war has not meant that the global trade in arms will end in the near future; and the processes of self-determination and democratization now occurring appear to be neither trouble-free nor irreversible. If we do indeed reach a total of two hundred members of the United Nations by the year 2000, some new countries will only be created by turmoil. Many will be created from the chaos associated with the breakup of empires (especially the Soviet-Communist hegemony and satellite system), and others will emerge from the divisions caused by long-repressed ethnic and religious strife. On the sidelines, extremists and terrorists will probably resort increasingly to terroristic weapons in order to obtain resolution of terms they judge to be favorable. They will undoubtedly apply pressure and perhaps resort to private armies in order to gain a legitimate political role.

Fortunately, this period is likely to be relatively short. Some isolated, lingering conflicts, such as those in Northern Ireland or among Palestinian Liberation Organization factions in the Middle East, may continue beyond this point, but their impact will be of declining regional and global consequence, and they will eventually solicit membership in the international system as the benefits of cooperation and integration into that system appear more appealing than the gains of vengeance. In the interdependent world sketched in the preceding chapters of this book, moreover, no nation will be able to conduct a lengthy war or build up monumental military forces to fight wars. Few, if any, will be able to satisfy the demands of their populations for freedom and economic prosperity by continuing to maintain the military establishments of this century.

In this respect, Desert Storm contained some important lessons about the economics and destructiveness of war. The total cost of the operation is now estimated by the U.S. Office of Management and Budget and congressional sources to have approached nearly $200 billion. Around thirty nations contributed to paying the bill. None alone had sufficient resources to shoulder the entire responsibility. The cost of war in the future is not likely to be reduced, and increasing numbers of countries may find themselves unable to afford the price of participation. This reverses a trend of the twentieth century in which wars were actually becoming more economical in current dollars as a result of the mass production and distribution of weapons, which lowered the cost of preparing to fight. In addition, many combatants could look to the United States or the U.S.S.R. to bankroll them and finance their wars once they were under way or had become more costly than anticipated.

The introduction of precision-guided munitions and other types of smart and stealthy weapons systems has proved incredibly expensive. The price tags for these increasingly necessary instruments of war—and the countermeasures to them—are not likely to decline (as was true with weapons in the past) because of the shrinking military-industrial manufacturing base. Until the 1970s, armies could rely on entire industries to supply their needs, and these products were generally available at increasingly lower unit costs as a result of diversity and competition among the producers. At that time, some companies could exist entirely on defense contracts and look forward to doing so indefinitely because the weapons being designed and procured had ten to twenty year lead times. Making weapons and other materials for war used to be profitable.

For the past several years, however, few defense contractors have shown significant profit, and the vast majority have reported losses; defense stocks have lagged far behind in equity markets; and some contractors' bonds are now rated as "junk." The end of the cold war in particular and weakened world economic conditions in general have caused shrinking sales and markets for defense contractors. The advent of smart weapons, coupled with rising costs associated with having fewer available producers, also means that armies on increasingly tight budgets have to pay much more for their weapons. Eventually, they will need to buy less to possess greater capabilities, but costs will continue to escalate unless more traders become involved. At the present time, unfortunately, the global arms trade seems very robust.

■ DOES FREE TRADE IMPLY MORE ARMS TRADE?
—Sandra Clemens McMahon

The end of the cold war has significantly altered the course of international relations and the corresponding defense strategies of most global actors. In response to the dramatic political transformations and the elimination of an Eastern bloc military threat, national defense spending and domestic demand have plummeted, and the economic motivation for manufacturers to seek new international weapons markets has escalated. On a global basis, defense industries have answered the challenge and adjusted to the conditions of declining domestic demand and overcapacity of production by intensifying and expanding global arms trade. Ominous prospects of deep industry recession, which still loom in the future, may serve to accelerate this trend. At the same time, nations and their leaders face the larger challenge of reconciling the economic needs of defense industries with their own national and global security interests.

Although extensive overseas marketing of arms often has the unfortunate side effects of proliferating modern weapons and encouraging precarious programs of collaborative production, most defense companies view such arms trade as essential to their immediate survival. In many cases, the wide dispersion of weapons production capabilities has resulted in the arming of our adversaries as well as our allies. Although many governments are presently supporting the effort to seek export markets, their endorsement stems from a variety of considerations, ranging from economic ambitions to compensate for domestic budget reductions or to alleviate development costs for new weapons systems through the collection of export revenue to political attempts to gain regional or international prestige by playing a key role in the defense industry. Only Japan has chosen to prohibit the export of weapons. Whatever the motivation for arms trade, governmental policies are shaped by increasingly conflicting demands and goals. Decisions to promote arms exports as instruments of foreign policy or economic revenue are tempered by the need to regulate exports in order to stop a dangerous arms proliferation or buildup.

Today, as a result of these economic pressures, a complex system of interdependent defense industrial structures is emerging on a global scale. This system has been constructed through a series of earlier friendly collaborative ventures in the production of advanced weapons systems and has been nourished by the liberal defense export policies of our European allies. In the past, these relations have been crafted from the sets of strategic corporate linkages between U.S. defense firms and their foreign counterparts in the advanced industrial states of Europe and Asia. Gradually, the cast of actors has expanded to include developing nations such as Brazil, Taiwan, South Korea, India, Turkey, Indonesia, Singapore, and Australia. As a result, the transfer of defense technology has become increasingly difficult to control, as numerous sources of capable defense industries and arms supplies have emerged and alternative sources for most weapons systems have become accessible around the globe. This scenario diminishes the power of major arms producers and creates a new set of rules governing the international weapons business.

Over the longer term, the pace of international arms sales will most likely decline. Since 1985, the macroeconomic environment, composed of elements such as lower military expenditures and declining procurement levels, has not been favorable to the defense industry. During the next five years, conditions stimulating the demand for weapons and creating new markets will continue to deteriorate. In recent years, the level of armament sophistication has been steadily elevated and the terms of trade have been gradually altered. In lieu of direct arms exports, the major arms producers are generally entering into coproduction and codevelopment arrangements that allow smaller nations to develop indigenous weapons industries and to eventually enter the export market as competitors. Consequently, fewer older weapons are now sold out of stock, and inventories are accumulating. In addition, microeconomic forces, such as the rising costs of weapons research and development, indicate future problems for the financing of armaments production and the long-term economic viability of many defense companies.

In the context of larger global objectives, several vital questions regarding the future of arms exports and technology transfers still need to be answered. With more limited resources available for defense, public policy decisions will naturally play a key role in determining which firms and, eventually, whether most arms industries themselves can survive. For example, as the principal arms exporter in the West, the United States is in a pivotal position and must decide whether to capitalize on its present advantage to pursue economic objectives by increasing arms exports or to use its influence to alleviate security threats by proposing a plan to curtail international commerce in modern conventional weapons and technology. We are facing the prospects of a dangerously heavily armed world in which control over the distribution of potent weapons systems has eroded. The acquisition of weapons and technology alters the balance of power in international affairs, and by freely and arbitrarily exporting such items, industrial states are supporting the ascent of potential renegade or terrorist military threats and the destabilization of entire regions. Therefore, it is crucial that U.S. policy balances and responds to demands of both economic and security objectives. Because governments are able to exert strong regulatory controls over defense trade, Congress should mandate stricter unilateral controls by expanding and strengthening the congressional approval procedures for foreign military sales and reforming the arms transfer process. In the end, however, because unilateral efforts are doomed to failure without the support of other powerful voices within the global community, multilateral restraint by the United States, Europe, and the Commonwealth of Independent States will be an essential factor in curbing the current pace of arms proliferation.

—Compiled from the following reports: Office of Technology Assessment, U.S. Congress, *Global Arms Trade: Commerce in Advanced Military Technology and Weapons* (Washington, D.C.: Government Printing Office, 1991), pp. 3, 5, 17, 28, 31, 35, 37. ∎

The expanded capabilities of smart weapons have added a new dimension to the considerations of war. Opposing armies now possess the ability to destroy specific targets and to remove surgically the industrial or military centers of their enemies. This stark reality may not prevent all war—or deter leaders from attempting aggressive acts—but the thought of such accurate retaliation and the increasing likelihood of such a reaction may substantially increase what is put at risk and give pause to those contemplating the odds of achieving political objectives through warfare. In fact, today's and especially tomorrow's smart weapons will probably achieve a higher level of deterrence than nuclear weapons have realized since the mid-1950s. Nuclear threats required those making them to risk their own annihilation and, thus, were increasingly perceived as hollow. While nuclear war promised a scenario resulting in possible mutual destruction for both the initiators of the conflict and their targets the smart weapons are more likely to deter aggression, since they are capable of accurate and specific destruction of targets, without extraordinary civilian casualties. Since they provide an option to complete annihilation, smart weapons are a more likely weapon to deploy and they constitute a more plausible threat. After all, it was probably not the threat of casualties or conflict with the United States that convinced Saddam Hussein to capitulate but that of the total destruction of Baghdad and the other centers of power and culture so important to the survival of the Baath party. The knowledge that future aggression will be met with a response that is devastating to the internal structure of a country—and not just one that involves some pain and individual loss of life—will contribute to the obsolescence of war over the longer term.

Will the world disarm? This, of course, has never happened. Many scholars have argued, in fact, that arms races have been more stabilizing than efforts (usually by hegemonic imposition) to achieve disarmament. By the twenty-first century, I envision a world in which many of the traditional incentives and capabilities that enabled nations to go to war will have been altered. It will be a world without empires and with fewer restrictive borders through which people and goods will be prevented from passing, particularly within regional areas. Interdependence will be a fundamental component of the management of the future global system.

In this regard, the expanding communications, cultural, and economic ties between countries and regions will promote such a high degree of interaction, collaboration, and mutual reliance that the momentary gains of using force will rarely, if ever, appear worth the significant risk to the system. Many social and ethnic groups will have achieved self-determination or autonomy within federal state structures, moreover, so that even the civil wars dominating our headlines today will be settled. The trend toward interdependence will continue as other ethnic conflicts result in the creation of several new, smaller countries that will find economic and security cooperation essential to their ultimate viability and survival. Finally, the industrialized as well as developing countries will be full partners in a global collective security system, whose roots were probably secured during Desert Storm. Clearly, the most notable achievement of that conflict was the formation of the coalition. The participation and cooperation of a broad range of countries in terms of their levels of development (let alone forms of government, ethnic makeup, and foreign policy) in response to the act of aggression and the contravention of the U.N. Charter were unprecedented. This voluntary display of unity suggests to me that now the potential exists to develop a global rule of law and a means to enforce it.

Consequently, the spirit that was exorcised in the sands of the Iraqi desert may have been far more important and powerful for the United States to have dealt with than the ghost of Vietnam. This spirit, namely, is the presumption that the international system, which encompasses such a wide variety of countries, was only effective when it was managed by great military powers and that these powers would act only when core values were threatened by events occurring inside their spheres of interest. Eventually, Desert Storm will be remembered for its lasting contributions to the global system and as a unified action by many countries (some of whose core values were not really threatened) offering help to a very small country that was believed to have an equal claim to existence. This right will come to be more universally respected, making the need for war less evident and justifiable.

Implications for the Emerging World Order

We should now return to the question of the design of the world order that is indicated by the decreasing utility of and resort to force. There are really no analogues with past international systems because each depended to a great extent on military hegemonies and superpowers as well as on the balances and tradeoffs that could be maintained among them for stability. In the world ahead, particularly the one imagined here, there will be many powers and many overlapping sources of power. The process by which power is created in such a system, moreover, will not be threatening or zero-sum. Inevitably, the balances that are achieved among the members—and the degree to which such balances will even be needed—will depend on how flexible and open-ended the international system becomes, rather than on the exclusive and specific nature of the terms by which new members are admitted and older ones change their status and situation. In many respects, the growth of global interdependence and cooperation will provide a framework of stability for all members by imposing a restraint on many forms of alienating or counterproductive activities within the system. In short, what's ahead allows for a future that is substantially different from the past, and one in which new rules and new tools will both come to be used in creating as well as maintaining order.

Global military forces will be downsized out of economic necessity, but they need not be less capable or able to act as a deterrent to future conflict. National military forces will most likely be reduced in size, will focus on accelerating deployability, and will eliminate much overseas basing. Military structures will concentrate on developing the ability to project forces rapidly, resupply them efficiently, and reconstitute them through a reserve system organization. A reduction in forward deployment forces will in turn inspire the development of superior indigenous transport capability, such as new cargo planes and ships. When the military capabilities of this streamlined model are fully understood, the new structure should serve as a further deterrent to aggression and conflict.

These are not at all gloomy prospects for the United States. What appears to be dawning is a system in which innovation and entrepreneurship will be highly regarded and rewarded and in which our ability to internationalize economic, cultural, and scientific activities will be a critical success factor in the effective linkage of the United States to the rest of the world. These new forms of linkage will replace most of the military or security alliances that the U.S.

had established previously in order to fight wars or to deter others from starting wars.

The resulting world order will not necessarily be simpler nor offer a danger-free environment. In fact, it may become much more complex. Multilateral negotiations and compromises are difficult to achieve. Responding to the political, social, intellectual, and economic challenges of international affairs will continue to be difficult and necessary, and so I do not expect that either our profile in the world or the activities of our government to promote U.S. interests abroad will decline substantially. But the institutional origins and tactics of U.S. strategy will change as the practice of basing U.S. military forces abroad is ended and the custom of using foreign aid as a supplemental form of military assistance—rather than as economic support for vital development in a broad range of countries—ceases. The biggest change will come conceptually. As we view the world as a less dangerous place, we will increasingly discover that what lies ahead contains far more opportunities than risks. This outlook will be especially fortunate for Americans because thus far, we have proved to be more skilled at capitalizing on the former than at devising ways to minimize the latter.

7

Circa 2000

The developments forecast in this book will probably not occur until well into the twenty-first century. But within that century's first two decades, I accept that our world will already be quite different in many respects from the one in which we are presently living.

The millennium will be a benchmark and will occasion much in the way of reflection on the state of the world—not as it has been but as we would like it to be. For this is an age of both new technologies and new possibilities. To some extent the process has already begun, as many political leaders have started to champion a set of issues (e.g., the environment, social welfare) they suspect will be key to attaining national and international positions of power in the elections and world of the mid- to late 1990s. Their political work and social consciousness-raising are helping to define the broad features of the international landscape as it will be viewed at the start of the next century and the challenges that will drive the system itself.

By circa 2000, the world will be characterized by three central facts: (1) there will be more people and robots on earth than ever before, (2) there will be less arable land and fresh water per person than at any time since these vital natural resources have been systematically measured, and (3) the surface of the planet will be warmer due to the accumulation of greenhouse gasses in the troposphere. The latter two phenomena may not prevail for the entire century, but every available current indicator suggests they will deeply and directly affect the nature of life on earth for the rest of this and probably at least the next decade.

The fact that the earth's population will have tripled by the start of the next century compared to the total population in 1900 will undoubtedly put the planet and its resources under great stress. Fortunately, such growth also provides us with a larger pool of intellect and with more minds to help solve the problems our increased numbers will create. Possibilities for progress may be limitless as the accumulated wisdom and creativity of so many people with extensive access to information and the freedom to pursue their instincts and interests are unleashed within the 1990s. In previous millennia, the significance of increased numbers was usually calculated in terms of the total impact on the rulers and the elites of having more slaves to shoulder the hard work of empire. Although they were free, these rulers and elites depended on and coveted the benefits they would ultimately derive from the increased production of an enlarged labor force that was not free. The cost to them was virtually nothing. In the next millennium, of course, we look forward to a world of free people in which all forms of slavery are extinct. We should also look ahead to a world in which there could be many millions of robots.

When envisioning the world's future work force and the functions and tasks people will be expected to perform, contemporary literature has not accorded a large role to or reflected high expectations for the future applications of complex, robotic machines. In today's world, only a few repetitive functions have been allotted to robots. In fact, the leading application areas for robots ordered in the first quarter of 1992 were identified as welding, material handling, and assembly. According to figures published in the May 1992 edition of *Robotics News,* the current U.S. robot population is estimated to be 44,000 units at an average cost of $106,150 per unit, and the trends show increasing orders of greater complexity—with unit shipments increasing by 10 percent—since the first quarter of 1991, and the dollar value of net orders increasing by 13 percent for the same period. A growing recognition of the competitive value of robotics also prompted an increase in international sales, which accounted for 31 percent of new orders.

Let me, then, make my bias clear. I think we need to imagine and prepare for a world in which robots will get cheaper and better and will come to replace human workers in dangerous, monotonous, and even very highly complex manufacturing as well as some service procedures. We should look forward to a day when humans will not perform most forms of manual labor nor depend on such categories of employment as a means of earning a livelihood. Consequently, we should begin to develop plans for occupational alternatives in order to guide the displaced work force in new directions. The solution to potential unemployment problems will focus on training people who have been replaced by robots to fill new jobs created by the evolution of industry. These solutions will have to be highly differentiated to take account of the categories of jobs robots will most likely assume and the humans they will subsequently relieve. The value of thinking about this now—and expecting that it will happen—is that we can possibly avoid the dislocations and trauma associated in the past with transformations of the character of the work force, of the needs of the workplace, and of the venues for making such changes happen.

World Politics Around 2000

What consequences will these developments have for the conditions of world politics and the nature of the international system circa 2000?

Before I answer this broad question, it is important to stipulate that I do not think the central facts outlined above will lead to radical or weird behavior in world politics. Unlike some curiosities of the last millennium, people will not repair to caves to await earthly catastrophes; new and fantastic religions will not be created in any significant numbers; nor will the people of the earth join hands immediately to establish world brotherhood or a world government. But the impact of these primary facts and the election of leaders to national and international office who are aware of those facts will create a closer sense of political community. This community will be based on the common need for all members of the international family to recognize the facts of our interdependence and the need to conserve the earthly resources we do possess.

Clearly, the period immediately ahead will demand genuine heroes as well as visionary leaders. Some will be the entrepreneurs who bring business and accompanying economic development to the countries now in transition to freer political and market systems. They will take enormous risks in doing so and will venture into areas and product lines the mainstream will have either rejected or never considered. Some will be top corporate leaders who will restructure enterprise. Others will be educators and social workers who manage and develop programs to improve the way institutions help people to learn and function independently. Inventors as well as scientists will also emerge as great figures as they experience that decisive moment of insight— or the patience to fail thousands of times before succeeding—and ultimately create new processes and applications that will solve human and social problems.

We will need such heroes. The future will not come easily, and the path will not be free of upheaval and risks. There will consequently be periods and pockets of tremendous yearning for old, familiar regimes and the safety of traditional systems in which the idea of freedom may be temporarily suppressed and the lives of individuals may be controlled rather than empowered with personal rights and privileges. Even the visionary leaders, who are most in tune with the forecast presented in this book, will not by themselves be able to inspire people to press their knowledge and creativity on all fronts to the edges that become curves rather than limits. Such leaders will need the support of ordinary people, who will come forward to perform extraordinary tasks and take exceptional risks in thought as well as in action.

Happily, such ordinary heroes will not be in short supply. The conditions of social and political life described in this book, which are now coming into view, actually arouse and otherwise reward people for taking the steps that expand frontiers, make us all freer, and apply the benefits of education, science, and technology well beyond the borders of any single nation or social group. Social or religious taboos prevent few remaining natural mysteries from being explored. Discoveries cannot be kept secret, and fewer and fewer persons involved in making such discoveries are motivated to conceal their findings. Furthermore, nations of the future will not have the option of isolation from the rest of the world. The hero's deed can be broadcast instantly around the globe, assuring that ambition and initiative will produce effects far beyond the immediate time and environment.

The increasing global interdependence will demonstrate the fragile nature of the conditions of life and trade we all share. This realization in turn will make us all much more aware of the role we play in creating each other's problems, as well as in solving them. At the same time, nations will be spending less money on weapons and the support of their military establishments in a world where the threats to security have substantially declined. The resources usually devoted to defense spending will increasingly be available for tackling environmental and societal problems, and by 2000, there will be a major redeployment of workers from defense industries and the armed forces to other enterprises and activities.

Such trends and developments will mean that foreign relations will be conducted through a large range of networks that cut across the public and private sectors, and that the central function of the international system will be to make sure that networking and transactions arise and flow freely. Overseeing this system of networks, of course, is fundamentally different from pursuing a systemic goal of preserving a balance of power or the geopolitical integrity and boundaries of states and empires. Furthermore, this new orientation will promote new goals. One of the accepted and globally recognized aims of the international system will be to promote the redistribution of wealth and power in ways that reflect comparative advantages and allow for universal growth. This in turn is how the trends forecast in this book will help both to lift the industrialized countries out of recession in the 1990s and to allow people living in the less developed countries access to global economic growth and developments in the next decade.

By the first quarter of the next century, moreover, teams of humans and our robots will have succeeded in creating a world environment and standard of living that can prevent needless death and suffering among the world's poor. Partly as a result of the application of science and advanced technologies to the current problems of maintaining food production and supplies in chronically impoverished places and for malnourished people, and partly as a result of better and more widespread communication about the causes of disease—especially those that contribute to such high rates of infant mortality in the less developed countries—for the first time in history, poor people everywhere could have equal access to food, safe water, housing, and medical care by about the end of the first quarter of the twenty-first century.

At this point a skeptic will ask: Who will provide these goods and services, and how will they be financed? In the past, and for most of the population of the Third World, only the family or the government was expected to be able to provide such basic necessities. In the future, the services of these institutions will constitute only part of the equation. Because several of the reasons people suffer shortages of safe water or of ample food supplies transcend governmental and village boundaries, the remedies will require the action of many different types of institutions. Regional and specialized agencies of international organizations, for example, may be more significant in providing water and food—and the means to increase the supplies of both—than will any current domestic government. Consortia of governments and businesses may also find themselves cooperating increasingly to assure that both the work force and consumers have the health and the means both to manufacture new products and to purchase them.

Another feature of this new world order will be what I call "continental drift." I put the term in quotation marks because I am not talking about the effects of plate tectonics but about the pushes and pulls that are likely to result in portions of one country forming sustained and substantial links with a portion of another country that far outweigh the bonds each maintains with a national capital. Even though we will still have countries by circa 2000, within their boundaries there will be considerable differentiation. As a result, trade flows, information networks, and cultural exchanges with parts of other countries will multiply.

In Asia, for example, it is not difficult to envision not only a genuine common market between the Association of Southeast Asian Nations (ASEAN) states but a de facto common market involving the coastal provinces of China and the countries of Korea and Taiwan. In South Asia, a similar evolution could occur for those adjacent provinces in India, China, and Pakistan and among them and some of the autonomous regions of China, as well as with the common market of the Southeast Asian states. Other parts of India may have more significant ties with markets and companies in the United States and Canada than with the states to which it is adjacent, especially if its vast reserve of human capital supports the development of a computer software industry whose products can be shipped and serviced by satellites. In the Middle East, such differentiation could take place as the people who share the region's great rivers make common cause and expand their trade and contact with one another in an effort to conserve what they have for all. But perhaps the greatest amount of such continental drift could occur in Africa, when in search of trade and economic growth, the countries near South Africa create a common market when a black majority government comes to power and countries in the northern part of the continent create strong trade links with countries in the Middle East.

Moreover, the advent of cheaper and faster forms of transcontinental transportation will accelerate the processes described above. Even more important, they will give rise to entirely new linkages that make good economic sense in the world of the next century but that we still cannot imagine in the present century.

One of the transformations I think lies ahead—though probably not until well into the next century—is an evolution in the nature of nationalism and a fundamental erosion of its impact on international affairs. Whatever the correct time frame of the eventual demise of nationalism, it is very difficult to imagine a world without the potent political force of nationalistic appeal, especially during a period such as this in which numerous conflicts have been sparked by long-repressed emotions and commitments and appear to have ripened from the seeds of nationalism planted in the early twentieth century.

The conscious attempt to secure the interests of one geographic or ethnic group over another—and to promote and enhance those interests, often to the detriment of another group—appears at first glance to inspire few of the qualities and values that are essential to the prolonged period of democratization, respect for human rights, and economic development I envision for the future. In the present century, entire countries and peoples have been destroyed in the name of nationalism. As a result, people today are still quite fearful that nationalistic sentiments, which have crippled nations in the past, cannot be adequately contained and that other forms of the phenomenon, which are emerging in the wake of the collapse of communism, will prove equally virulent. However, in the decades ahead, these fears will subside. Most likely, the nation- or ethnic-centered conflicts we are now observing and the others that will probably occur during the remainder of the 1990s will mark the last vestiges of the phenomenon rather than signal its staying power for the future.

By the first decade of the next century, world politics will begin to be played out against a background in which the concept of nationalism will have been largely removed as an impetus to conflict. Forces seeking self-determination and those opposing it will both have been reconciled by shifting focus to a larger regional or international picture. As an indirect result of this transformation, leaders will no longer be forced to base their political platforms on choices or policies that substantially benefit one domestic group by severely hurting or constraining the interests of another. In part, this will occur because most members of the international system will insist on it—we will all be living in a world in which the conflicts of the past will be considered archaic, far too costly to pursue, and far too threatening to the stability of the system of interdependence through which world trade will be conducted. There will also be much less reason for appeals to nationalism in the first place. Particularly if my forecasts prove correct, the large number of new, smaller nations that will be created in the period ahead and the subsequent search for the appropriate geographic expression of their identity will result in all groups feeling less threatened by the existence of others. Rather than fighting to repress particular groups or to determine which groups will gain supreme power in a multi-ethnic country, more countries will reflect the diversity of the world's population and will simultaneously reflect the absence of any vested interest by superpowers or regional hegemons in maintaining the status quo on world maps.

In short, world politics in the next century will be determined by a conjunction of forces, most of which will be in conflict with and therefore intolerant of nationalism. In addition, the support for nationalism will have been much reduced, if not eliminated altogether, as people everywhere come to value the benefits of their interdependence and, consequently, increasingly adhere to the principles outlined in the Universal Declaration of Human Rights.

At the moment, my colleagues have cautioned me to hedge my bet on such prospects. However, to do so would also mean rejecting any significant change in the vision of internationalism. If nationalism were to thrive, it would in essence impede the evolution of a new form of international society and politics based on something different from the nation-state and obstruct the vision that human nature will encourage such a development. To accept such premises would mean, however, that we have entirely overlooked the promise of the future. We cannot discount the impact that the end of both the cold war and the types of conflicts that once generated superpowers will have on aggregate populations and on their perceptions of how best to secure their interests; we also cannot overlook the power of both these developments to change fundamentally the way we view ourselves and our relationships with each other.

I could be wrong. Since the dawn of nations, there has never been a time when people have rejected the concept of nationalism or sought to retard its growth and appeal. But the striking characteristic and promise about the world of the next century is that it could be unique. It may be not just a little but remarkably different from the present era due to the free movement of people, ideas, goods, and capital. This suggests not only that the age of nations may be past but also that the value of thinking in such nationalistic terms to explain motivations for people to work cooperatively or to fight with one another may have sharply declined.

Ideas and Their Consequences

As people live better and longer lives, they will also accumulate more knowledge. The free flow of information will increase the availability of education and the numbers of people who can take advantage of it. Thus, education will become a universal process through refinements and innovations in communications technology and global distribution of the knowledge via low-cost information retrieval systems. Currently, only a tiny fraction of the world's population has access to a college education, and wide disparities exist among countries in the numbers of such students that can be accommodated. In China, for example, there are fewer seats in all of that country's universities than in the universities in the state of California.

By circa 2000, this will have begun to change significantly. Universities—especially those in the United States—will belong to the world. There will be more universities and more seats in them throughout the world, but there will also be larger numbers of foreign students in schools in North America and Europe than at present. The great centers of learning that exist on these continents will have made the transformation from state and class institutions to world learning environments. In the future, our present concern with the large and growing numbers of advanced degrees and patents given to foreign students compared to Americans will be replaced by a concern that we ensure that our centers of advanced learning fully reflect the global nature of our links and trade as well as the diversity of the planet's population.

The activities in our universities will reach more people. In part, we will revise our methods of teaching students and tailor our curricula to the pace of individual learning. Right now, more than two-thirds of the lessons taught in U.S. colleges are repetitious. They echo lectures and presentations of the previous year and the last several decades. A professor of economics or history still teaches this year's students about the laws of supply and demand or the origins of World War I by repeating last year's words and offering the same insights and explanations. Students still take notes that they throw away after the exam, and all students are forced to learn at the rate the information is given rather than at the rate they could potentially absorb such knowledge. Sometime during this decade or the next, we will shift substantially to computer-delivered tutorial courses to provide such basic information and theories and to allow students to learn at individual rates. When this technology becomes widely available, we will hold the means to transmit such learning around the globe and allow professors to develop much more specialized or advanced courses for smaller groups of students. Some businesses like IBM, which every working day instructs more than twenty thousand employees in a classroom or other learning environment, are already using such advanced educational techniques, with a record of great pedagogical success.

The idea of the classroom will also change as we improve the ability to transmit our books, voices, and images across thousands of miles. The technology of telecommunications and the advent of practical and low-cost satellite videoconferencing will allow learning centers to operate overseas campuses and programs and to reach an even wider foreign student population. In addition, they will provide alumni with constant resources and opportunities for continuing education. In the process, most countries will revise educational requirements. For example, in the future students may spend less time in college (e.g., three versus four years) and more time in graduate school and in continuing education thereafter.

Now, the most exciting aspect of these potential developments is not the provision of better education for the same type of student but the involvement of larger numbers of students in the learning process altogether. All administrators of international higher education programs have agonized over the cases of students from poor countries and poor families who are admitted to programs with tuition waived but who ultimately cannot afford the travel and living costs to attend. The kind of future I am sketching here would solve these students' immediate problems. They would not have to command the resources to travel thousands of miles and the funds, once at the school, to afford to live and eat in order to partake of education. They could do so even in a remote village.

Such developments will also hasten the end of dictatorship. The dynamics shaping the international system outlined in this book will make it increasingly difficult for the few dictatorships that currently exist, as well as those that might come into being in the countries where democratization temporarily fails, to do so in the future. Realistically, it may be difficult to construct systems of free markets and democratic political processes simultaneously. Consequently, for a period of time, some nations may tolerate a phase of benevolent dictatorship in order to maintain stability while the economic structure is undergoing drastic revisions. The idea of freedom, as we have learned, cannot be effectively suppressed, and the ability of dictators and command economies to reap benefits from world trade and development is substantially declining. As a result, even though the reasons for the rise of dictators to positions of power may not be altered or eliminated, their ability to remain in power will be slowly eroded by economic trends, technological progress, and the expansion of educational opportunities. Coupled to this, moreover, is the plain fact that with the end of the cold war, countries such as the United States have a diminishing need to maintain relations with the leaders of governments that violate human rights. Furthermore, such political figures no longer have the option of turning to a friendly Soviet Union to underwrite their dictatorships.

On the whole, dictators do not surrender power easily or depart gracefully from the scene. Nor do the members of the entrenched and loyal social groups that brought the dictators to power and on whose largesse they have come to depend participate willingly in a process that empowers others and reduces their own fortunes, status, and holds on power. Nevertheless, there will be fewer dictatorships tomorrow than today, and probably none will exist by the end of the first decade of the twenty-first century. Those who have previously come to power and managed to retain strict control by denying the expansion of political participation and repressing human rights are among the oldest living political leaders today; in part, therefore, my forecast will come true through the natural action of the grim reaper. In most circumstances, we have also learned that dictators do not govern effectively or well. They make mistakes and tend to execute self-serving policies that obviously enrich their clan and support groups but that greatly impoverish the bulk of the people in their countries. In the future, neither armies nor crowds are likely to be tolerant of such decisions, especially in an open information environment in which the beneficiaries of government actions are widely recognized and condemned by the general public and the consequences for victims are highlighted.

Although some of the remaining dictatorships will end only with the violent overthrow of the incumbent, most will be terminated by agreements reached between the incumbents and their opponents to form coalition governments or to reform constitutions and hold national elections, as has recently been the case in Chile, Taiwan, Argentina, and Thailand. In the end, the remaining dictators have discovered individually that they cannot hold on to power indefinitely and that they stand a better chance of enjoying its fruits if they take steps to enable themselves to retire diplomatically, before they are buried by the masses in a state of ignominy. So, for a time, the new world order will also include conditions and political transitions that will make ex-dictators feel safe as well as obsolete.

None of the foregoing implies or necessarily ensures that the world will become a more equal place as its people become freer and its markets more open. What I foresee is a world in which everyone is free to live and work and move and in which no right or opportunity is denied anyone as a matter of law or other type of government policy. It was the absence of these freedoms that inspired turmoil and revolution in the past millennium, and correcting this deficiency is precisely what will make the twenty-first century one of unprecedented peace, social stability, as well as political freedom.

There will still be large disparities between rich and poor people, and the poor will continue to vastly outnumber the rich. But the rich will not be perceived as achieving their status by repressing the masses, nor will they find it in their interests to amass or maintain their wealth by doing so. In addition, poor people will no longer assume that opportunities to improve their status do not exist or that their children will be unable to achieve better and healthier existences than they are presently able to realize. Each class of society will be able to hope as well as think that such improvement is possible and that social progress is the proper objective of governments as well as of private enterprises.

In fact, by mid-century equality of opportunity will be available to all regardless of residence, color, or national origin. With this development will also come the recognition that we do not all have equal abilities and that these differences, rather than the artificial boundaries drawn in blood or by the arbitrary and capricious acts of dictators, account for the luxurious life-styles of some and the poverty of others. However, to be categorized as poor in such a world does not have to mean (as it does now) that people live in misery without hope for their children or dignity for themselves, in constant fear of attack by hunger, disease, and crimes of violence. What I envision is a term of ample economic growth and development and sufficient programs of concerted action by public and private institutions to eradicate these plagues and provide equal opportunities for all citizens to live and work to their fullest potential.

It should be possible to achieve these goals over the next twenty-five to fifty years. There are no mysteries about why people die from diseases that can be prevented by small applications of medicine, improved water and sanitation, and the provision of information about the sources of sickness. There is no secret yet to be discovered about how to eliminate hunger and, what is more important, about how to teach people to produce and distribute more food; enough food is already produced in this world to eliminate hunger on a global basis, and there is no longer any good set of reasons to prevent such freedom from hunger from occurring. There is no magic rite that has to be performed to create jobs and train people to work well in them. As economic recovery gathers momentum, millions of people of all ages will be going back to work.

Theoretically, there is no real limit to how many people can and should work. A truly global demand for goods and services is just beginning to be appreciated and no one can yet come up with an accurate estimate of the potential for economic growth this represents. But consider this: In the twentieth century, more than two-thirds of everything that was bought and sold was acquired by less than one-quarter of the population. In the next century, we are looking at a customer base, in terms of world population, that is many times larger than the base that existed in 1980 and that will want a range of goods that encompasses virtually everything producers and growers are able to make. We tend to forget this potential for increased consumption in our preoccupation with the high end of the market and the challenge of competing with the Japanese for high-tech customers. But in the next century, most of the world will still want and need very basic commodities that we are all capable of producing (although some far less expensively than others). There is nothing wrong with aspiring to sell a billion Bic pens in China, a billion aspirin in Russia, or a billion light bulbs throughout the Commonwealth of Independent States. Each such sale would generate trade and improve the lives of the sellers as well as the buyers. Sitting in the United States (or Tokyo, for that matter), we frequently forget that most of the people in the world possess far less than we do and still need to acquire reliable supplies of very basic and simple products. At least initially, the growth in world trade that I envision will come in the so-called old-fashioned way: through entrepreneurs creating products of good quality for people who want to purchase them.

Religious Revival and Reflection

No forecast of the immediate future would be complete without addressing the one body of thought that through the ages has specialized in anticipating and designing the future: namely, religion. An exhibit at the Smithsonian Institution's Museum of Natural History in Washington, D.C., reconstructs an early Neanderthal burial place and portrays the ritual that appears to have been associated with death. In this exhibit, a corpse has been prepared in a special manner, stones arranged in a distinct pattern, and the dead provided with a supply of ancient animal fur and bird feathers. Of course, no one actually knows what this meant. But the circumstantial evidence strongly suggests that from the first, humans had invented or were inspired to invent forces that transcended their own lives and power on earth. It seems as though from our earliest time on earth, we have understood that there were forces well beyond our control and reach and have felt the need to interpret our fate under these circumstances.

Acknowledging the existence of such supernatural and uncontrollable forces inspires most of us to act and search beyond the realm of worldly experiences on a scale that far outreaches normal requirements for life on earth as solitary creatures or as part of some larger group or broader society. The Neanderthals apparently did not casually discard or forget their dead, for example; nor do we. The earliest written accounts of history reveal that primitive humans had the need to worship gods, a need that has hardly diminished with time or with even the most advanced technologies and insights into our physiological and psychological makeups.

Over the centuries, although countless tribes, states, and empires have risen and also fallen from power, the empire of religion has been much more stable and long lasting. Today, there are popes, patriarchs, and imams who trace their lineage to divinity; there are Buddhist monks who believe and can convince hundreds of thousands of others that they are the reincarnation of a god. But the only present-day king who can trace his existence to a bona fide deity is the emperor of Japan. In contrast to the scope of powerful religious figures, this ruler has little actual influence and exerts it over a small number of people.

Historically, for thousands of years before Christ and for the two thousand years since, people have done extraordinary things in the name of their religion and have made extraordinary sacrifices of their own earthly needs and desires for the sake of the god or gods in which they believed, and they will continue to do so in the future. In a world that is increasingly free, in fact, more people may choose to believe in one religion or another or to invent entirely new ones. As a legacy of Communist repression, as many as a third of all people in the current global society may not yet know what religion has to offer or may have been taught or otherwise coerced into disbelieving. Yet, despite the history of restraint, the fastest-growing social movements in China and Russia today are those associated with religion.

The key question to pose now, therefore, is what role religion will play in the creation of the future forecast in this book. As I suggest above, I think the global numbers of religious adherents are likely to increase; however, religious beliefs will be characterized by much more individualism and common sense rather than by orthodox tenets that are stoically and centrally mandated by church or state. In the past, religious beliefs have appealed to many individuals in free societies, and the collapse of communism has liberated many individuals and offered them an opportunity to explore the tenets of religious faith. For instance, if religious freedom spreads within such vast nations as China and the former Soviet Union and the new believers indoctrinate the next generation, the numbers could spread rapidly. By the middle of the twenty-first century, our world may contain a higher proportion of religious believers than at any time in the past. At a minimum, the numbers could be staggering. At the same time, the concept of freedom will be emphasized in the realm of religion to parallel the aspirations for freedom in society as a whole. Consequently, traditional religions will be constantly modified, and new religions will likely also emerge.

Some religions—such as those of ancient Egypt, Greece, and Rome—have been founded on terms and by people who were particularly committed either to the state as they knew it or to some form of international order. Others— led by individuals such as Moses, Christ, Mohammed, and the Gautama Buddha—have tended to create trouble for princes and established authorities and have defied the state to search for equity and greater freedom. They called on humans to act according to a set of laws, values, and dynamic forces that were consistently at odds with secular authority and the local and global regimes they were attempting to establish. In the time of Christ, His actions and message led His followers to rebel against and ultimately shatter the Roman Empire. In our time, we have seen the power of a religious figure cause millions of people in Iran to reverse the course of their development and topple one of the strongest modern dictatorships.

Most likely, no one who was involved will forget the dark days during and the errors of judgment that preceded the fall of the shah of Iran and the ascent to power of the Ayatollah Khomeini. Other than the Vietnam War defeat, this is probably the most traumatic event to occur since the so-called fall of China in the 1940s. The aftershocks of the event significantly disrupted and altered the course of U.S. foreign policy. Throughout the multiple crises surrounding the shah's fall, the creation of an Islamic state that declared a holy war against the United States, and the imprisonment of U.S. diplomats as hostages for more than a year, American decisionmakers and those who supported them (including me) consistently underestimated the power of religion to move people to do things that seemed greatly at odds with their interests. We failed to see in part that this is precisely what religion is all about—that is, giving people reasons and the strength to do things that cannot and should not be measured in secular terms.

So, the fundamental certainty about religion in the future is that when mixed with politics, it has awesome power. If this power is applied constructively to international affairs, it will impose moral requirements on the actions and decisions of leaders. The power of religious convictions, however, may also prove to be a destructive force in international affairs if it is used to promote discrimination or to justify aggression. It enables people to reject both modernization and interdependence for the sake of creating societies that conform to doctrines, teachings, and preferences that are based on values and goals completely out of the mainstream and adverse to the forces discussed in this book. The Ayatollah Khomeini, for example, had written extensively on what an Islamic state would look like if he were to come to power in Iran, and his followers developed their revolution with a specific blueprint in mind. In other words, religion can create states and governments.

Another certainty is that the political leaders produced by religious forces act differently and are motivated by different factors than the leaders we usually encounter. They may want to participate fully in the emerging world order or to ignore completely the details and distractions of the global interactions. Not every religious head of state in the future, consequently, will be as worldly as Pope John Paul II or Father Aristide of Haiti, and not all church leaders will feel compelled to keep their empire and its laws and requirements separate from those of the states in which they reside.

The final certainty is that religions and religious leaders benefit as much from modern communications and the expansion of political participation as do secular politicians. Their messages get further and have greater impact thanks to the radio and television pulpits they enjoy, the desktop publications they can easily and cheaply produce, and the instant feedback communications systems can provide.

All of this does not suggest to me, however, that the world of the next century will be swept by religious movements and the proliferation of fundamentalist states. There will be some such states, but they will still be relatively few in number, and the religious movements will produce comparatively few national leaders. Part of the reason for my thinking this is that in the period ahead, most religions and their leaders will be very busy with their new status and with the large body of recruits and faithful to which they will have to minister. Also, and short of the creation of new, messianic religions around the time of the millennium, I think the existing religions— with the possible exception of some sects of Islam—have decidedly turned away from the mission of exporting revolution or converting unbelievers through state-sponsored coercion.

However, threats to international stability still remain. One such threat is ingrained in the trend toward the regionalization of religious affiliations. Such alliances transcend national boundaries and may espouse principles that are contrary to the universal norms and definitions of ethics. Menacing groupings, such as an aggressive, fundamentalist Islamic alliance in the Middle East, may provide an obstacle to developing cooperative global spirit and undermine the seeds of democracy that have been planted in the regions.

At another level, the religions of circa 2000 will still be very far behind the times. They will have done relatively little to help people cope with societal changes or the dislocations these will involve, especially for the urban poor. Religion will also fail to appeal greatly to the group that is likely to be the most empowered in the next century and from which much of its leadership will come—namely, women. No major religion currently treats women with equality; none allows women to lead it; and those with the greatest mass appeal in the developing world seem to be the least inclined to give women such rights, power, or status. More than any other set of facts or conditions, this will constrain the influence of religion over world politics and limit the spread of its influence and appeal much beyond present boundaries, even in countries where a close identity between church and state currently exists.

The world of the next century, finally, will also exhibit far less repression of any sort than did the world of the twentieth century. The fact that religion can be practiced freely in all states, in short, and that people can choose to believe or to remain on the periphery without fear of reprisal by any organized government at any level will remove the need for some religions and religious leaders to secure their positions through control of the government apparatus. Whatever else religions try to accomplish in the emerging world order, consequently, they will not be required to expend the political efforts so typical of past eras in which they were compelled to etch out a position in the society by controlling the monarch in power.

What I am saying in essence is that occurrences of the rise of such figures as the Ayatollah Khomeini—who, after all, had the need to achieve power because he was exiled from the country that contained the religious center with which he identified most closely—could be far less frequent in the twenty-first century than at any other time in history. If this proves to be the case, the role of the state as the earthly articulation of the kingdom of God will substantially decline and eventually disappear. And all of this might well occur at a time when more rather than fewer people find hope, dignity, and real meaning in their beliefs and in their ability to have them—and to profess differences in them—without incurring or needing the intervention of governments or armies.

Who Will Be Leaders?

What character will the leaders of the early part of the next century have, and what experiences will they bring to office?

Considerable change lies ahead in the overall profiles of persons who will be elevated to positions of national government and international business leadership. Their characteristics and background will not necessarily fit the molds of our contemporary leaders. Even more fundamentally, we will need to think about an entirely new class and pool of talent that will be available and mobilized to achieve power. For most of human history, the leaders of nations and empires have been men. Yet about half of the world's population has been female. As a result of a substantial shortage of skilled and educated labor sources within industrialized economies in the next century, countries and business enterprises of all sorts and scales are increasingly likely to be run by women. In the early part of the century, women leaders will continue to be trained in a manner similar to that of their male counterparts because we have relatively little experience with institutions and procedures devoted exclusively to preparing women for public or private business leadership. However, by mid-century, I suspect we will have invented new ways and processes to train women aspiring to reach the top of political and corporate ladders and that this will underscore the special qualities and wisdom women bring to issues and problems that require decisions. Moreover, we will all probably live a decade longer than we do now, so we may be in much less of a rush to abandon the resources people with fifty to seventy years of experience will bring to situations of leadership and problem solving. Retirement will be pushed back several years, and the wisdom of age will gain renewed respect within Western society. This trend will also allow women (as well as men) more time to have and raise children without feeling so acutely that devoting time to a family will eventually make them less competitive in the professional world and much less likely to attain top positions.

The path to power, consequently, will be not only longer but fundamentally different. The gestation period for leadership will be longer in some cases, and the entry points into what might be considered leadership tracks will be more numerous and much less linear. People will be able to pursue two and even three careers and bring to leadership positions a much broader range of experience than at present. And fewer people will come to power, especially in those countries that will have completed the transition to free markets and political systems by the end of the first quarter of the century, without sufficient training or preparation for leadership. Those who created what they consider to be revolutions will not necessarily be those who make such transformations possible. And those who bring their countries and organizations through transformations may not necessarily be those who will lead those countries and organizations in the next phase of their development. The good news in all of this is that leadership resources are expanding. There will be a larger source of potential leaders at different stages of societal development than we have been accustomed to drawing from in the past.

The process by which one leader succeeds another will also be increasingly different in the future than it was for most of the world during the present century. Constitutions and the process of orderly and legal governmental changes will create conditions in which coups d'état will be rare occurrences and in which opposition groups will come to power based on well-developed and well-publicized programs of alternative national strategies rather than on demagogic appeals. Conditions of interdependence will serve to enforce universal legal and democratic standards. As people everywhere gather more knowledge and gain access to more free information, they will be more difficult to manipulate and more discriminating in their judgments about what present and potential leaders should promise and can deliver. Eventually, those seeking leadership positions will be forced to develop additional ways of receiving direct feedback from constituents instead of relying nearly exclusively on the advice of pollsters as they develop their political platforms and campaign appeals.

Most likely, all of the above will not occur in the first ten years of the new century. But the point of making such predictions is to raise the possibility that the quality of political life and the nature and supply of leadership at all levels and sectors will be transformed sometime during the era ahead. The main ingredients for such a transformation already exist, and more will be supplied by the constructive economic and social conditions that will emerge as more of the globe is governed under democratic processes than at any time in history.

8

Conclusions

A motto for my building at Georgetown University is inscribed above an auditorium entrance. It is a passage from the philosophical works of the late Jesuit father Pierre Teilhard de Chardin. In March 1931 he wrote: "The age of nations is past. It remains for us now, if we do not wish to perish, to set aside the ancient prejudices and build the earth." It is a good way to think about our changing world order.

As I have tried to show in this book, the emerging dynamics of international politics have never been more likely to produce the will to realize Fr. de Chardin's vision than they are in the period ahead. Anyone contemplating the opportunities unfolding in the next century ought to ground his or her thinking in imagining that sometime between 2000 and 2025, the goal of ending many ancient prejudices will have been accomplished. The result is likely to be a new order based on much more inclusive principles than any that have hitherto been used to organize the international system. Subsequently, a new sense of ourselves and of the planet we are all responsible for maintaining coupled to the recognition that our destiny lies beyond the nation-states we presently inhabit is likely to evolve.

The future will not come easily. But the ideas and forces shaping it represent the most powerful conjunction of positive forces for peace and development that I can recall when surveying other epochs in international affairs.

Despite the considerable talk in Washington about the advent of a new world order, however, a clear vision of the components of such a structure has not yet been realized. The policies that will be capable of translating hopes for peace and imaginings about how to achieve it into reality have not yet been fully devised, and the end of the cold war has not necessarily made the world a less dangerous place. In fact, a short period of considerable upheaval lies ahead. Consequently, the world map will almost certainly change, and some cases of national fragmentation are likely to occur. The ethnic and religious conflicts so much in today's headlines may result in the division of countries ranging from India to Israel. Geopolitical changes will occur practically everywhere as the residual conflicts from the colonial and cold war eras are finally resolved.

Although some cases of fragmentation may come initially in the aftermath of ethnic or religious conflicts, the demands of economic and political survival within the framework of increasing global interdependence will inevitably encourage integration. In the future, the greatest amount of change will result from relationships that grow out of trade and technology. The forging of economic and then political unions, which for many states accomplishes that which cannot be achieved independently or in isolation, will become the vehicle of the next generation of world leaders in obtaining security, legitimacy, and prosperity. In the process, democracy will become practically universal as a form of governance because it is only through free choice that people share what they possess in the hope of improving the future for all. So, after a relatively brief period of turmoil, we are likely to enjoy the longest period of peace, respect for human rights, and economic development in history.

The Central Role of Education

Whatever happens, education is at the core of the process because training a new generation of leaders is vital to the successful construction and maintenance of a new world order. U.S. universities will have to teach people about changing national conditions and international transformations at a time when no one thus far seems to have predicted current events or their rapid pace of development.

In one sense, the customer is way ahead of the manufacturer. Young people want to know what is happening in the world, why, and what it portends for their future. For most of the 1980s, the fastest-growing undergraduate major at U.S. universities was in the field of international affairs. And typically, it has been this growing corps of internationally minded students that has pressed faculty committees to develop more offerings that explore the economic as well as technological and environmental dimensions of today's key global issues. The number of students studying foreign languages has also increased, along with the proportion of each class that opts to spend a semester or two abroad. At no time since the end of World War II or the polarization of college campuses over the Vietnam War in the late 1960s have college students been as interested in foreign affairs as they are today.

Beyond the challenge of interpreting current events, educators have an obligation to begin writing the history of the future. Our starting point ought to be the cardinal theories that nurtured us and the reasons they failed to forecast what has happened. Consequently, we need to share with students our sense of wonder and puzzlement at the current course of events and to analyze the weaknesses in our anticipation of these developments. In this time especially, the classroom can and should become a laboratory looking at the experiments in democracy that fail and others that succeed and where accurate and meticulous reflection, observation, and reporting of results are primary goals. Students and instructors should be as excited as those who are trying to debunk cold fusion, develop a vaccine against AIDS, or look beyond "quarks" and "wimps" for new forms of energy and grand unified theories of the cosmos.

The best approach to describing what is taking place is interdisciplinary. Few professors are trained and educated in two or more disciplines, however, and most have attained tenure and have published as a result of increasing specialization. This specialization makes it difficult for professors and students alike to comprehend how the economic causes of perestroika also imperiled President Gorbachev's ability to sustain the political changes he initiated as a result of invoking the reforms. Similarly, before we can explain the actions nations take over such matters as protecting stratospheric ozone or altering global warming trends, we need to understand the role of ozone in the atmosphere and the reasons for scientific uncertainty—until very recently—regarding the chemicals that cause its depletion. A host of other environmental issues presents similar conceptual challenges, yet these issues cannot be ignored in teaching about world politics or be relegated to back-burner status because (as we used to argue during the cold war years) it is much more important to devote attention to the chemistry and statistics that indicate the balance of power between the United States and the former U.S.S.R.

In an interdisciplinary atmosphere, there is a greatly expanded role for the study of history and ethics in courses on international affairs. Professors and students of the 1990s are not the first humans to experience systemic change or threats to an entire ecosystem or even change of the sort that shakes one's basic notions about power and justice. Discovering how humankind coped with such challenges in the past may provide valuable clues about how to do so now—or about which pitfalls to avoid (e.g., religious fanaticism and tribal warfare).

Finally, classroom lectures and their lessons should incorporate qualities of intercultural sensitivity. All cultures respond to change differently. It is important to understand which mixture of conditions and culture may lead to stress and conflict at the human as well as societal levels. This is particularly important in an era of what my late colleague O.B. Hardison termed "global consciousness" (in his book *Disappearing Through the Skylight: Culture and Technology in the Twentieth Century*, 1989). This phenomenon is activated when communication devices allow information to reach many different kinds of people, practically without regard to their location or political system, and when machines, once their function is learned, impart certain values and techniques of mastery over the environment. A factory worker in China or Czechoslovakia or a farmer in Poland or Panama suddenly have much in common. It does not matter whether they are aware of this metamorphosis. What matters more is that they have acquired access to the tools that facilitate economic transformations and political revolutions—that is, machines that allow them to produce or grow more or act faster—and have formulated the idea that this knowledge should somehow improve their lives.

The American Response to Change

Americans are traditionally a generous and compassionate people and we will be no less so in the period ahead. Many of us have not travelled far, in generational terms, from the trauma and dislocations associated with the rapid political and economic changes of the past century. And virtually all of us know our roots lie in many of the countries currently facing such fundamental change. We worry about the fate of refugees from Haiti and the elderly people standing on lines in Moscow or Warsaw waiting for milk or bread. We are appalled at the violence and slaughter associated with coups d'état in the African countries that house our ancestral roots. We have not yet become inured to the photographs of children in Bangladesh and Somalia with distended bellies caused by hunger and chronic malnutrition or to the videos of babies stuffed three to a cot in Third World hospitals and clinics and for whom there is inadequate medicine and health care.

Unfortunately, we are trapped in a period of frustration over how to tackle these problems and eliminate the causes of these conditions. We have a sense that our aid programs in the past have done little to make the world of the urban and rural poor a substantially better or less dangerous place. Neither national nor international leaders or organizations seem to be able to come forward with imaginative and cost-effective programs to ameliorate the plight of the poor and also provide them with the means to break out of the downward spiral that appears to have imprisoned them. We have totaled up the bills for past aid, and we shake our heads at the impossibility of procuring comparable amounts for aid today. We are also deeply worried about the condition and health of our own society and the limited resources available to improve our own people.

During my last period of government service, I took part in the preparation of weekly briefings for the president on world events and the threats they posed to American security. Over the past several years, I have often speculated as to the nature and content of such a briefing if it were focused on the subject of America's current internal problems. For example, in every seven-day period in 1992:

- Fifty-five hundred persons lost their jobs and 1,376 businesses went bankrupt (according to the U.S. Bureau of Labor Statistics and the U.S. Bureau of Economic Analysis).

- One person was robbed every hour (based on statistics via U.S. media).
- On an average night one million of our citizens spent at least one night in jail; six hundred thousand were homeless (according to the U.S. Department of Justice and National Resource Center figures).
- Approximately one child in every five lived in poverty and one-quarter of the nation's children went without immunizations (based on National Center for Health Statistics, U.S. Department of Health and Human Services).
- Seventy-seven hundred students dropped out of high school (according to the Center for Educational Statistics).
- Eight hundred fifty persons were killed in automobile accidents.
- Nearly two hundred Americans were murdered by handguns.

These statistics would prompt most heads of state in the Third World to think and react as if their country were under siege. Yet for the most part, we have not turned inward, isolated ourselves from the rest of the world, or neglected the plight of others within our global community. Instead, we are in search of ways to change these conditions, both at home and abroad. In the past, it was quite a bit easier to formulate a popular plan of action because there were clear domestic and foreign threats to which we all agreed we should respond. Moreover, response to these threats usually did not involve apparent tradeoffs between defense and foreign affairs versus domestic growth and development because the government budget was able to grow without generating a deficit or imposing substantially new and much higher taxes. Public works cost less, and our population was smaller, younger, healthier, and exposed to far fewer known risks to health and safety. Today, the reverse is true in every case.

In order to make a difference in our own society and in the world, consequently, we will have to choose our goals strategically and our approaches economically. I think this will translate into confining our actions to a much narrower scale and stage but with a concurrent commitment to increasing our success rate. The stimulant/catalyst here will be the so-called "peace dividend" accruing from the end of the cold war. In reality, it will be far smaller than anticipated and will evolve over a much longer period than initially suspected. These key considerations will inspire our leadership to define national goals more clearly and outline our approaches to achieving them more precisely. Most likely, we will move in the direction of targeting problems and assuming that if we discover a way to solve them at home, we will also be contributing to their elimination abroad. This concept would also promote consensus-building about the nation's foreign policy. Within this framework, the general public will more readily accept the need to finance and share the work toward solutions that serve a national interest that in turn is increasingly affected by developments beyond our borders because people would be much more aware of the integral relationship between domestic and international problems.

We will probably never return to a cold war mentality, which was characterized by a clear national sense of the threat and need for international action. The threats and dependencies of the future are too complex and subtle; so is the makeup of our country. But we will not retreat from a complicated and interdependent world in the 1990s and beyond, any more than we would have withdrawn from a simple one in which we were confident about our global power and responsibilities. We will just approach it differently and with more of an eye for reconciling what we need to accomplish at home with what others would like us to achieve for them abroad.

Viewed from this perspective, the current search for a catchword or turn of phrase to replace "containment" and thus ease the process of discovering and building consensus is bound to be quixotic and quite unnecessary. There is no single comparable threat to U.S. interests—and we are no longer the kind of people or government that is capable of acting the way we did in 1946-1947. We are, however, increasingly able to comprehend the world of complex interdependence in which we are living, and we will fashion imaginative responses to it. These responses will probably defy labeling and will vary extensively with each unique situation, and they will certainly not come easily at first. But respond we will.

Future developments in world politics may tell us if we have indeed exhausted the ideas that have inspired and pushed people to change the systems under which they are governed or the forms by which governments surrender a bit of their sovereignty for some greater good or objective. The vital role of institutions and universities today is to prepare farsighted and compassionate citizens, students, and leaders who are able to stimulate and manage change.

The Importance of Vision

Imagining as well as coping with what's ahead will require leadership with a vision of national as well as global politics. Presently, however, democratic political systems do not seem ready to provide this variety of leadership. In Europe, for at least the remainder of the 1990s, many of the leaders who achieve power in the industrialized democracies will have been shaped and selected largely by their successes in fighting and ending the cold war rather than their experience in designing the policies needed to deal effectively with the aftermath. These leaders may also be accustomed to focusing on domestic problems and remedies for the state of decline in their societies and for the conditions of a recession that began in the late 1980s and will not be fully over until the mid-1990s. Most likely, this traditional mind-set will not inspire many to bold, new approaches to world politics. In America, the election of Bill Clinton and Al Gore represents a sharp break with the past; the president is the first graduate of a school devoted to the professional study of international affairs and the vice president is a leader in according global environmental concerns top priority in foreign relations. So if vision comes from anywhere, the source could well be U.S. policy.

Nevertheless, many of the key global issues discussed in this book will remain on the back burner, and neither politicians nor their electorates will be much inclined to jeopardize their futures or shift significant amounts of resources to deal with them. And the process by which most political leaders are empowered will keep attention focused on what must be done at home rather than shifting it to what could be accomplished abroad—and in partnerships with others—and how such a broader vision would be in everyone's interest. The states that are being created out of the collapsed multiethnic empires will also generate leaders who are intensely occupied with highly localized issues and problems. Consequently, leadership of the variety required to reach beyond these preoccupations will be rare for the better part of the 1990s, until people gradually come to realize that their needs can be better served by men and women of broader vision and by regional as well as global networks.

We are already aware of the downside associated with the inevitable revolutions and evolutions in the name of democracy. The democratization process is even now producing its demagogues and its racists, who have managed to gain access to power. At the same time, it allows so many self-interested voices to be heard about what ought to be done, especially in the economic arena, that this flood of public opinion discourages thorough thought about which policies will work in the long-term picture and how best to implement them. There is, consequently, a tendency to think the answer must lie in choosing among the many popular options put on the table rather than in asking what is missing and, in some cases, choosing a necessary but unpopular path in the short term.

All of these trends and complications, however, will eventually stimulate much greater strategic thinking and planning on the part of leaders. For the short term, there will be a gap between what today's and tomorrow's leaders are capable of doing and what the political and economic dynamics sketched out in this book will require them to do. From Russia to the United States, contemporary leaders are needed to preside over the dismantling of huge defense complexes and industries in ways that do not foster depression within their economies and to find alternate jobs into which defense workers can be successfully deployed. New economic plans are needed to assure that peace dividends are realized and that the returns are productively spent and well. New social and political arrangements need to be constructed that allow a much broader range of social forces and ethnic groups to engage in political participation in their societies and yet assure the formation of governments that are able to make collective decisions—some of them very unpopular, such as raising taxes—that will facilitate the operation and competition of free markets, both nationally and globally.

Eventually, the evolution of the international structure will require leaders of a different sort than those we have been accustomed to visualizing and electing. Such figures will be adroit both at shaping policy and at staying in touch with the needs of the people and the hardships they face. It will take some time before sufficient education and training are available to prepare these leaders as well as to create the conditions that allow those grass-roots representatives who are in touch with the masses to come to real power. In the process, these leaders will also develop the professional and personal networks that will enable them to build the coalitions and other rudiments of legitimacy that may later be required when calling for national and individual sacrifices. The leaders of tomorrow will also have a much better understanding of the dynamics and causes of the problems they are facing than those of today and the recent past. They will be able to speak authoritatively to people across generations, social classes, and cultures about the range of problems and issues that affect the quality and the future of their livelihood. In short, the leaders of the new century are just now beginning the process of their formation as the old methods and verities are demolished and future leaders are cut free to think, plan, and hope about fulfilling expectations that are only beginning to manifest themselves.

In all of this, U.S. leaders will play a central role. For what will not change substantially is the degree to which people everywhere look to this society to lead, to inspire, and to devise solutions to current and future problems. No matter where one stands in the debate over whether the United States is in decline or the rate at which it may actually be rising, no one doubts that the world looks to Americans for support, in spite of what may or may not be occurring. Some groups in some societies may have less respect for us than others or may find themselves increasingly at odds with our policies and practices, but they nonetheless turn to the United States to gauge their progress toward and control over the future. The future, in this sense, still belongs to Americans, and it will first dawn here.

Our challenge will be to live up to these expectations, to heal our own society, and at the same time, to do so with generosity and compassion for others. This is still very much within our capacity and our reach. We are still a force to be reckoned with—one that is powered by steady virtue, and one that will lay claim to a mission and remain deeply involved in changing the world order to allow all people to participate in our accomplishments and share our dreams. Long after the changes and forecast discussed in this book have played out, U.S. participation in and support of a new international order will still be among the key ingredients for its success, and Americans will still be playing a major role in securing future progress and assuring equal distribution of the benefits to the widest possible extent. For the nation we represent is composed of a wide diversity of people and forces that have never tired of imagining the future and how it could make the lives of all better and more free.

Implications for American Foreign Policy

What will the changing world order mean to Americans? World orders have changed before without making substantial differences in the lives of many other than the elite, and profound changes have taken place in the past that have been isolated from the reactions and influence of ordinary people. This time and in the era ahead, things are likely to be different. People everywhere do have a growing sense that they will be greatly affected by the international actions and responses of the United States in particular and that this response may have a substantial impact on individual as well as global security and prosperity.

By the start of the next century, Americans will be fully conscious of their position of deep involvement in and dependence on the surrounding world. For our future livelihood and well-being depend on our ability to sell our goods and communicate our ideas on a global basis—and without interruption by costly arms races, geostrategic rivalries, or wars. This sense of internationalization extends far beyond the current concern about corporate competition with industries of Europe or Japan; it requires a new pattern of comprehensive thinking and planning in global terms, not simply confining this thinking to narrow sectors of the economy in which foreign markets are needed and large profits are expected. Similarly, we need to be more deeply vigilant and concerned than ever about the causes and resolution of conflict because an outbreak of hostilities in any region of the globe could directly affect our welfare at home.

More so than during the cold war, in fact, our future growth and well-being require the ability to search for and seize opportunities wherever and whenever they arise and to prevent violence and aggression across a broad range of issues and on every continent. We cannot, as we once did, prosper or survive in isolation from the rest of the world. Eventually, this realization may not necessarily inspire another U.S. century, but it will certainly result in a century in which Americans will benefit most from what's ahead.

What then is the role of the United States in a such a new international structure? This will be the central question of U.S. foreign policy for the remainder of the 1990s. Indeed, it is this issue—rather than the ones that surfaced in the debate in the 1980s over whether U.S. power was in decline—

that will define the parameters for our continued global involvement. Our most fundamental role will be to assist the emerging leaders in a wide variety of countries in the management of the societal and political changes discussed and forecast in this book and to guide them to select the policies that will ultimately transform their economies and political systems into ones that are genuinely free.

Ironically, I found this was envisioned as our destiny even at the height of the cold war. Carved into the entrance of the small park built in honor of President John F. Kennedy by the commonwealth of Massachusetts adjacent to the Harvard campus are some lines from his inaugural address. As I read them to my teenage son, my voice broke for just a moment. JFK's words, I found, had power to move me still; I think they moved my son as well. The quotation over which I stumbled was vintage Kennedy: "Now the trumpet summons us again—not as a call to bear arms ... but a call to bear the burden of a long twilight struggle ... against the common enemies of man: tyranny, poverty, disease and war itself."

Hearing these words again, when the world situation seems so profoundly hopeful but the challenge no less demanding, I thought the late president would have been pleased to know he was right. America is still very much involved in listening and acting with imagination and compassion.

Advice about what to do and how to protect U.S. interests in international affairs in the era ahead is hardly in short supply these days. Two former presidents have spoken out extensively, and a legion of my colleagues have written books and essays about the need for continuing U.S. engagement in the world and the importance of having our actions influence the distribution of power and the fate of the new countries and problems being created. Unfortunately, for much of this decade our leaders will remain preoccupied with the tough domestic issues, which are partly the result of our enormous investment in containing the Soviet Union, and the transformation of U.S. businesses into truly multinational and global enterprises, which make a profit by employing fewer workers to generate products or locating sources of cheap labor and resources (and not necessarily in the locales where they originated).

Yet, we need the world and the world needs us. Our problems cannot be solved by actions taken solely within our borders. Similarly, government and private revenues cannot grow without devising a strategy to make our products and services competitive on a worldwide basis and without taking some steps to assure that the evolution of the international system is a peaceful process, thus eliminating the need for substantial rearmament of either the United States or the countries of the former Soviet Union. Inevitably, all of us in this enterprise will amass a wish list of things we hope the U.S. government will be able to achieve in this decade in order to improve the chances for the kind of future I am forecasting for the next century.

My own list begins with the need to anticipate and tackle the problems associated with the breakup of empires, ranging from the Soviet Union's in central and Eastern Europe to those of the European powers in the Middle East, Africa, and Asia. This venture involves far more than the disaster-type relief we have been contributing to those countries making the transition to free markets and political systems or our continued readiness to intervene when their unwillingness or inability to settle conflicts leads to war. Such aid and reassurance may still be needed, but our support should not stop there.

The political conflicts of the postimperial and post-cold war eras are apparently not going to be solved by themselves. As our repeated frustration with attempts to bring the Arabs and the Israelis to the negotiating table attests, we need to go beyond process in these types of conflicts and, working with other countries, develop concrete formulas for solutions all sides can focus on and subsequently build the necessary domestic support to embrace. We also have to be prepared to permit the new countries created in the process to benefit from free trade. How will we react as these new countries become involved in world politics and start making and exporting goods and services that compete with our own products? Clearly, we need to proceed beyond the present global trading framework constructed under the GATT to allow these new countries not only to enter the world market but to do so on terms that allow them to prosper while protecting our own interests.

In the past, we have done very poorly in this area. As many countries followed our advice and sought to enter the world economy by responding to consumer demands for low-cost, high-quality goods, we have responded by complaining that dumping rather than development has occurred. At some point in this decade, all of the countries that started the transition to free markets in 1989-1990 will produce goods and offer services that will represent jobs lost to Americans. We need to anticipate this development, avoid the remedy of protectionism, and find ways to assure that our own labor force can be redeployed to skills and enterprises that produce goods and services the rest of the world will still demand from the United States. Now, I cite this example because it illustrates the close relationship of foreign and domestic issues and problems in the period ahead and highlights the importance of developing policies that consider economics as well as politics and that balance our domestic and international objectives. The point is that no foreign policy can ultimately be successful without taking these complex relationships and needs into account.

Such international activity will require a substantial improvement in U.S. diplomacy. For a variety of reasons that have been discussed extensively in professional and academic circles, the nation's encounter with other governments and cultures was episodic, arrogant, and largely reactive for most of the 1970s and 1980s. This development should come as no surprise to a country that substantially reduced its spending on and commitment to international affairs training in recent years and at the same time deeply politicized its foreign service.

Today, there are few genuine professional diplomats, and their career prospects are not broad or promising. U.S. embassies often function as postboxes for the myriad federal agencies that play a role in shaping our activities abroad—something that is not necessarily bad—but they do so without reference to overall strategic planning or direction—something that is hardly effective or desirable. Our representatives encounter cultures and people who are not familiar to them. Many times, upon arrival at a post, our diplomatic representatives lack sufficient knowledge of the language or customs. They may not have an educational background or enough experience to comprehend the dynamic forces shaping that nation's interest, as well as ours, on the international scene. And we have neither the funds to attract and maintain a high quality of foreign service nor the resources to allow our diplomats abroad to effectively promote U.S. interests, products, and culture in imaginative ways. In this regard, student or professional exchanges are important steps in international training. Until its demise, the Soviet Union provided one hundred times as many scholarships for foreign students to attend its universities as did the U.S. government, private universities, and foundations combined.

Globally, the U.S. diplomatic, commercial, and cultural presence has also faded. Less money is available for the conduct of foreign affairs than ever before; morale is very low within the U.S. Foreign Service; and interest in entering such a career is declining among top students. As a result, we are entering an era of perhaps our deepest involvement with and interdependence on the outside world armed with far fewer knowledgeable persons and the financial resources to support them than at any time in our recent history.

■ NEW DIRECTIONS FOR THE U.S. FOREIGN SERVICE IN THE TWENTY-FIRST CENTURY
—Sandra Clemens McMahon

How should professionals working in the global community respond to the challenges and opportunities of the post-cold war period? This question pervades virtually all areas of international affairs career planning since the first rock was chipped away from the Berlin Wall and a new era in global relations was inaugurated. Answers require both introspection and reorientation.

A recent conference at the State Department addressed this issue in relation to the role of the U.S. Foreign Service in the year 2001. It was hosted by the Institute for the Study of Diplomacy at Georgetown University and attended by past and present members of Congress, the State Department, other agencies, academic institutions, and private industry. According to a report that summarized the results of the conference, the participants envision a global future consisting of complex relationships, nation-building, economic competition, poverty, and widely diffused power. Within this multifaceted atmosphere, they speculate optimistically that the United States will have the potential to prosper, assuming that its institutions are capable of responding to the diversity of challenges ahead.

According to the conference report, the U.S. Foreign Service will have a greater role in the future global scene. A combination of factors supports this claim. Isolationism will no longer be an option in the interdependent world of the twenty-first century. In addition, populations and leaders of new as well as old democracies will be likely to employ the classic diplomatic tools of representation, negotiation, analysis, and communication in order to advance national interests through persuasion and compromise rather than intimidation and aggression. International and regional organizations, such as the newly revitalized United Nations and other regional and technical forums, have also advocated the use of diplomacy in international relations. However, in order to fulfill this enlarged role, the U.S. Foreign Service must adapt to the new conditions abroad, with increasing numbers of actors in the international arena, and at home, with decreasing government resources, by adopting the same "lean and mean" management techniques used by successful private sector firms.

The strategic vision of the State Department in 2001 is both geographical—government to government—and that of coordinator of the specific functional activities of the government when an international component is involved. In order to function as such a nucleus of governmental activity, the Foreign Service would need some strengthening and housecleaning. Given the availability of many human assets and the record of underachievement in the Foreign Service, the report compares the organization to "a pantry full of choice ingredients for a feast without a recipe book." The conference participants recommend that the effectiveness of the Foreign Service can be increased by the application of five steps of simple reorganization: Exhibit more willingness to experiment with new approaches on a small scale, exhibit more flexibility in hiring all levels of qualified personnel, provide more training and enrichment of existing personnel, delegate more authority to empower personnel to contribute to their full potential, and provide fewer bureaucratic obstacles to thwart efficient output. Such modifications would improve the resources and streamline the structure of the U.S. Foreign Service and position it to assume a leading institutional role as the government it represents attempts to cope with the demands of a complex and challenging global system.

—Compiled from *The Foreign Service in 2001* (Washington, D.C.: Institute for the Study of Diplomacy, 1992).   ■

Reversing these trends toward false economies and disengagement will not be an easy task. There is a sense in the United States today that the end of the cold war—like the end of every other war—will enable our forces to come home, our global presence to be reduced, and the money spent on foreign affairs to be redistributed at home. Legitimately, there are some very compelling reasons to think this way. No American can survey the current state of our society and feel secure or content. Our infrastructure and public works need repair and upgrading. Our educational system needs an overhaul and a recommitment to excellence. Our people without homes need a chance to find housing and to secure the jobs that will eventually finance housing. Those without medical care need a practical and affordable system to supply this basic need. And those who are hungry need food. In considering these fundamental problems, it is hard to blame those who contend that we should not be developing aid programs to build schools in Bulgaria, clinics in Romania, and food distribution programs in Russia unless we have finished the job here at home.

Government in the 1990s, of course, will be compelled to find a way to do both. The fate of other countries and peoples is as important to U.S. security as that of our own population. Whether we want to or not, we have to work simultaneously to provide help to those in need abroad as well as at home. One lesson we have learned over the past fifteen years is that the problems and discontents of other societies take very little time to reach or threaten our own, and they may have severe repercussions.

Restoring hope and human dignity at home should be our top priority. There is no secret as to how this can be accomplished, only substantial disagreement about the root causes of current problems and the most cost-effective remedies to be employed. I believe it is pointless to debate the causes much longer, especially when we have done so little in the way of experimenting with the remedies. At some point, to have large populations of restless hungry and homeless in our cities will require immediate and concerted action to give these people hope and food. By the end of the 1990s, we will commit ourselves to eliminating the sources of these problems in the United States. We should accomplish this before returning to the moon, building a space station, or planning a manned space flight to Mars. If there is to be a peace dividend, it will most likely be earmarked for this purpose and cause. When the resources it generates fall short of solving the problems, a tax on all imported fuels may have to be levied to make up the difference.

Improving the character of the U.S. presence abroad and the understanding of what is going on may be subsidized by getting out of the foreign aid business and using the resources spent on so-called development assistance for diplomacy and the promotion of specific technical assistance. Half of all U.S. foreign assistance is presently funneled to Israel and Egypt. It has promoted development in neither country and at the neglect of needs in many others. Such investments were necessary when the cold war raged. Now, it is up to the countries themselves to solve the domestic problems that have led to wars and in turn retarded the investments by their own people and governments that would typically promote development. The United States has much to offer the rest of the world in the period ahead in the area of education and with ideas on how they can help themselves. The bloated bureaucracies that propose and oversee the distribution of foreign aid (and that cost more than a quarter of the aid budget to maintain) are obsolete. They do not add the value or wisdom we will need to help others and help ourselves in the complex period ahead.

Finally, we need to develop a consensus about international affairs that stresses the opportunities more than the risks ahead. This will probably prove to be the most difficult of the challenges we face in thinking about the future because it will require both vision and strategy. We have had such a consensus in the past largely because there was a clear and present threat—that is, the Soviet Union and its policy of exporting revolution—to which all agreed we should respond. Undoubtedly, as the system has evolved, the threats today and especially tomorrow will be more diffuse, and differences will arise over the justification for responding to them at a time when controversy is also mounting over the share of our scarce resources that should be spent at home rather than abroad.

Constructing this consensus will also be demanding. It will require a greater degree of compromise and negotiation. In the past, our foreign policy was the result of coordination and cooperation within a very small political and economic elite, virtually all of whose members were on the same wavelength about what needed to be done and why. Today, a larger number of people have divergent opinions about our role in the world and possess the means and power to influence political decisions. At the same time, many more people comprehend that our actions in foreign affairs directly affect the quality of their lives at home. Currently, no elite group has offered a set of solutions to the problems we face on a global scale, and there is little, if any, consensus within expert circles or the body of general opinion on the sources of many of these problems or the most cost-effective solutions.

As a result, the United States has approached the construction of a new world order inconsistently, with hesitation, and without projecting a strong sense of confidence to people at home or abroad to assure them that we have a long-term plan in mind. The global community has observed that our initiatives to aid former Communist states founder, our help to emerging democracies under challenge or siege varies greatly, and the rhetoric that is necessary to win elections contains alarming notes of protectionism, isolationism, and insensitivity. Different foreign policy courses are advocated by each branch of government, and the executive branch and the legislature have not been able to agree about the priority, shape, or funding of even one initiative growing out of the immediate end of the cold war. These divisions and disputes are reflected widely in public opinion polls, which suggest that our electorate wishes to reorder our priorities and presence abroad but cannot find the common threads that allow enough people to unite on a course of action it is willing to finance.

How, then, in these circumstances can a consensus be built? Probably only the presidency commands the attention and resources needed to perform the job. So, executive actions during the decade will be crucial in preparing for the twenty-first century. Part of this time, of course, will have to be devoted to rebuilding domestic strength and rectifying the social problems that have plagued so many of our citizens, caused our educational system to fall behind the systems of other countries, and prevented many of our industries from regaining a competitive edge. But parallel to these efforts, we must also plan a dialogue focusing on how our engagement in the world—and the developments that take place as a result of it—can build our national and global strength. In order to conduct a genuine dialogue, foreign policymaking must be removed from the small rooms at the White House, State Department, and Defense Department and be separated from the specialists in government and even academia. Decisions must engage a broad range of national and local leaders from all parties and all branches of government as well as private industry in setting new goals for our actions and leadership in the world and developing new tools for the conduct of our foreign relations.

In other countries, this work is done by the permanent bureaus of political parties and the shadow cabinets of the opposition. In the United States, our parties do not have such an extended and substantive existence between elections. Most of their management time and resources are consumed by paying past debts and raising funds for the next election. Our great think tanks also no longer have the capital or the time to engage in this type of dialogue and appraisal because they are increasingly required to produce research that serves the immediate needs of their corporate and philanthropic donors. Obviously, a void exists that can probably only be filled by presidential initiative and leadership to frame U.S. world policy.

Part of what will be required to make this effort successful is the mandate to look well beyond current constraints and problems in planning our future foreign policy. This is vital because we need to anticipate the momentum and the changes that are ahead. In contrast, our tendency in the past has been to think and act as if the future were a function of linear extrapolations from the present. These calculations have resulted in policies that served us well when the threats and our resources were relatively constant but not when we were faced with fundamental changes and declining resources for international activities. Taking the longer and broader view will require both imagination and a commitment to setting goals to define the characteristics of a world order from our point of view and to developing the most effective methods of shaping that vision in light of our own domestic needs and preferences.

There is another equally important but less obvious reason to develop such a long-term view and set of goals. In spite of whether we wish to bear this burden, the rest of the world still looks to the United States for leadership and direction. Other nations may not want to follow our advice or take our direction in the end, but their leaders do expect that we will speak and act as an example to other nations. The present drive toward a new world order, after all, is something they see as "made in the USA," and from our earliest annals of history as a nation (*Novus Ordo Seclorum* appears on the Great Seal of the United States), we apparently have been intent on creating such an order. Thus, others look to us for goals and definitions—or at least a process for articulating them. We should be as ready to provide such vision in the post-cold war era as we were during the contest with the former Soviet Union.

We will also work much more closely with a broad range of nations in the period ahead, and we cannot assume that they will be willing to follow our strategies blindly without some sense of where we plan to head. This incentive for cooperation was less necessary during the cold war because the threat of a common enemy generated a united opposition. At this time, the consequences of opposing U.S. initiatives were grave, and our ability to secure concerted actions was aided by the visibility of Soviet adventurism. But now— and increasingly in the future—we will be undertaking consultations with countries that will not necessarily be inclined to follow our lead. They will have to be persuaded not only that we have established firm directions and goals but also that their interests will be served as well as ours in working together with us.

At a practical level, we will have to change many of the methods as well as the ideas that underlie our foreign policy. The key tools will be coordination and consultation, for example, and this new strategy will require that U.S. diplomats utilize multilateral forums and organizations more frequently in order to develop support for the approaches to international issues and problems our government will endorse. We will have to become more comfortable as a host of or participant in high-level international conferences in which we cannot necessarily control or forecast the results. In addition, we will have to listen more attentively to foreign opinions about how particular problems should be solved and issues handled. All of these adjustments will not be easy for a nation accustomed to the loyalty of its allies and to setting the agenda for international affairs. Nor will the adjustment be easy for our leaders, who have tended to measure the success of a president or a secretary of state in world politics in terms of individual achievement and notoriety. Leaders have been identified by what they have named personally (e.g., doctrines) and accomplished directly rather than by the processes of international cooperation and conflict resolution they have taken a part in initiating but then not dominated.

In a thematic sense, the new world order emphasizes processes and ideas that involve many more players and, consequently, much greater variety in approaches. In the long run, this will be very desirable for a country like the United States, which has never sought the role of nor been comfortable acting as the world's policeman. Instead, other nations should arise with increasing frequency to take initiatives to solve regional problems and conflicts. Their doing so will enhance the likelihood that such solutions can be found and made to last and will substantially reduce our own exposure and risk in the process.

So, I foresee a future in which America remains a great power but also in which the United States is required to exert less effort to maintain a stable international order because the one that is emerging represents values and procedures of global appeal and significance.

The Future Beyond Us

Imagination will be especially important in the future. Whatever we think the next century holds, for example, we tend to conceptualize it in terms that relate to events and developments on planet earth. Yet, perhaps the most exciting dimension to our future is the prospect of discovering that we are not alone in the universe. On Columbus Day 1992, scientists in the United States began to search the entire sky for evidence of unusual electromagnetic radiation in the microwave spectrum that could be the first indication of intelligent life elsewhere. To date no such evidence has been found, nor have even our most powerful telescopes and satellite observatories confirmed the existence of planets of any sort in other solar systems. Even recent indications that two to three massive and possibly planet-like objects may be orbiting a pulsar (PSR1257+12) some 1,300 light-years from earth will take years to confirm, as the gravitational effects of these objects on each other are in the process of being studied.

But the possibilities are awesome. Astronomers now estimate that some 100,000,000,000,000,000,000,000 (10 to the 22d power) stars exist in the universe; 400 billion are in our own Milky Way galaxy alone. If only one out of a million of each of these stars had planets in orbit around it, this would mean that as many as 10 to the 15th power planets could exist. In short, the chances that we are not alone—or that in the 17 to 20 billion years that the universe has existed, other intelligent life-forms have developed—are far higher than those suggesting that we are the only intelligent life-forms that could have developed in any time and in any place.

By the end of the 1990s, in any case, we are likely to know much more about the universe and our place in it. We are likely to have heard sounds amid the static of space coming from distant sources in the universe that do not conform to any known signature of the noises associated with the Big Bang, pulsars and quasars, or the elements that currently make up the periodic table. We have not heard such noise before, partly because we were not listening on a continuous basis and partly because the equipment used to analyze radio signals we could detect was not capable of effectively discriminating among all 300 million channels in the microwave spectrum. Between Columbus Day 1992 and mid-decade, National Aeronautics and Space Administration (NASA) and Jet Propulsion Laboratory (JPL) scientists will have built powerful enough multichannel spectrum analyzers to accomplish such eavesdropping.

What will it mean to the human race to recognize in our lifetime that when we look up at the night sky, the great and cataclysmic forces of creation have bred life and intelligence before us in variety? We will probably gain little insight into the sources of the radiation we detect or discover whether the intelligence that generated it still exists because space-time distances are so vast that signals from one galaxy take millions of years to reach earth, even traveling at the speed of light. In a certain sense, humankind has been preparing for such knowledge for millennia. Every organized religion, in its doctrine and gospel, anticipates that life and intelligence exist throughout the universe.

I suspect our first reaction will be to develop a deeper appreciation for and awareness of our humanness. There will be renewed inquiry about what it means to be human and mortal as well as considerable debate over whether the previous efforts we have made to communicate with other intelligent life-forms through radio broadcasts, golden compact discs placed aboard the Voyagers, and golden plaques affixed to the Pioneers should be substantially altered. The writers of science fiction will probably have a chance to widen their circle of fans, and television programs and talk shows will treat the event to the same prime-time coverage that only the *Apollo* moon landing and the *Challenger* disaster have previously received.

Over the longer term, the discovery of other intelligent life in the universe will probably focus much more attention on preserving our own civilization and less on building a machine to transport us in the direction of another suspected form of intelligent life. For the next twenty-five years, the main activities of most national space programs will be the management and conservation of earth. However, it is the scale and design of space-time that will capture our imagination. We will probably think that our life-form is rare. We will also know more about the process by which planets are destroyed as well as created. Ironically, the knowledge that others exist—and may have ceased to exist as the stars that powered their galaxies extinguished themselves—will make us ever more mindful of the tenuous hold we have on existence.

And the Future Within Us

The ideas discussed in this brief history of the future have the power to induce us to set aside most ancient prejudices and many modern pathologies. The building of the values, institutions, and procedures to safeguard earth—and give humankind a special place in a universe of tantalizing complexity and variety—now lies ahead.

With all that has happened, the approaching millennium is perhaps an appropriate time to reflect on the values and qualities that make us human—and on whether there is anything that lies beyond both history and ourselves. My late colleague O. B. Hardison thought we might well evolve—or something else would evolve—to become more intelligent or even independent of the carbon basis of our life cycle. As silicon computer memories, "we" might last longer or indefinitely, if that were our goal, and our knowledge and presence might "populate" the universe in ways that even the most creative science fiction writers have not imagined.

The twentieth century, by and large, is not one in which we should take exceptional pride. Unfortunately, the political and economic forms we developed in this century have not prevented war or genocide nor engendered universal equality, health, or general well-being. A considerable portion of what we have to offer the history of the future about ourselves is yet to be discovered. We have the potential to achieve the goals mentioned above and more, and we now have coming into view a world order that might actually lend itself to pursuing advancements for the good of humanity rather than for wealth, dominion, and security purchased at the price of repressing others.

It will be hard to resist the instincts of the cave. We are suspicious of and hostile to strangers; we take enormous risks to protect our young but not those of others; and we will feel most uncomfortable and vulnerable as we release and renounce the means to make war, which we maintain in order to protect our core values and priority interests. The environment also poses threats that—although many are of our making—lie beyond our control now and that will affect human populations and settlements differently. We may not identify readily and charitably with the plight of others living in polluted air and near toxic lakes and rivers. But there has never before been a time when the incentives for leaving these instincts and reactions behind have been greater. Unlike our predecessors, we cannot help but be aware of the global consequences of retaining such instincts and the costs of acting to advance only our own immediate interests. We have seen wars—and studied others—that leave nothing to the imagination about their horrible and enormous costs and toll on soldiers as well as civilians. We have also seen cruelties enacted routinely on both massive and small scales by ordinary people in the name of ideas and objectives that suppressed our more noble instincts.

But history and imagination make a difference. We are a part of all that we have been. We also have the capacity to dream about what might be and act based on what it is we want to become. As a result, we have used knowledge to revolutionize political life, create wealth, move mountains, communicate with the stars, and make the future different from the past.

Appendix: What Happened, 1981-1990

1981

Reagan becomes U.S. president
Reagan assassination attempt
U.S. closes Libyan embassy
Reagan orders production of neutron bomb
U.S. and Egypt sign agreement on nuclear cooperation
American hostages released by Iran
Perez de Cuellar elected secretary-general of U.N.
US/USSR nuclear arms reduction talks in Europe begin

Poland imposes martial law
USSR/Japan trade pact
USSR/Vietnam 5-year aid agreement
USSR/West Germany sign Natural Gas Pipeline Agreement
Greece becomes 10th member of EC
France and Egypt sign nuclear cooperation protocol
Mitterrand elected French president
Pope John Paul II shot by Turkish terrorist
Attempted coup in Spain

Israel attacks Iraq's nuclear reactor
Morocco and Libya restore diplomatic relations
Saudi Arabia and Libya restore diplomatic relations
President Sadat assassinated in Egypt
Saudi Peace Plan for Middle East introduced
Gulf Cooperation Council formed to safeguard regional stability

China reduces military spending
Marcos ends martial law/Reelected as Philippine president
India and China normalize relations
Khmer Rouge offensive against Vietnamese in Kampuchea
China announces food shortages/Appeals to U.N. for aid

U.N. sponsors conference on Namibia
Zimbabwe establishes diplomatic relations with USSR
Mozambique joins COMECON
Senegal and Gambia unite to form Senegambia

Duarte becomes president of El Salvador
Border conflict erupts between Peru and Ecuador
Isabel Peron freed in Argentina
Antigua becomes independent
Belize becomes independent
Cancun summit on north-south relations

1982

Britain approves Canadian Constitutional Act
Argentina invades Falklands
War erupts between Britain and Argentina
Panama takes control of canal based on 1978 treaty
Nicaragua and USSR sign 5-Year aid pact
Right-wing leader D'Aubuisson elected in El Salvador

Brezhnev dies
Andropov elected general-secretary Soviet Communist party
Polish Parliament dissolves Solidarity
Greenland votes to leave the EC
Spain becomes 16th member of NATO
NATO agrees to deploy Pershing II and Cruise missiles by 1983

Israel invades Lebanon
Lebanese president Gemayel assassinated

India and Pakistan sign economic/cultural 5-year pact
South Korea proposes reunification talks
Chinese streamline bureaucracy
Japanese government approves increase in military spending

US relaxes restrictions on trade with South Africa
Habre takes over power in Chad

Senegambia confederation created by treaty between Senegal and Gambia
Syria breaks off relations with Iraq
Iran invades Iraq/Iraq bombs Iran in Gulf war

1983

Walesa wins Nobel Peace Prize
US successfully tests Pershing II and MX missiles
Reagan describes USSR as "Evil Empire"
US/USSR sign 5-year grain agreement
USSR suspends START negotiations
US troops invade Grenada
Lebanon civil war continues
Attack on US Marine barracks in Beirut
Begin resigns/replaced by Shamir
US Embassy in Beirut bombed
Syria expels Arafat

USSR/Angola sign new arms agreement
USSR/Egypt trade agreement
South Korean airliner shot down by Soviets
Demonstrations in Europe against NATO missile deployment
Greece-USSR sign 10-year economic pact
Pro-Solidarity demonstrations in Poland
Poland announces 3-year austerity plan
Martial law ends in Poland

U.S. Cruise missiles delivered to Britain
Socialist prime minister Soares elected in Portugal
Craxi elected Italy's first socialist prime minister
Kohl wins in West Germany
End of military rule in Turkey

UNITA guerrillas shoot down Angolan airliner
Hindu-Muslim riots in India
Aquino assassinated in Philippines

State of emergency declared in Peru
Unemployment riots in Brazil
Ortega presents 6-point peace plan in Central America
Protests against Pinochet in Chile

1984

US withdraws from UNESCO
Bishop Tutu wins Nobel Prize
Andropov dies/Chernenko named successor
Soviets withdraw from Olympic games
Soviets deploy SS-20 missiles in Baltics
Soviet astronauts return after 237 days in space

France and USSR sign 5-year economic pact
EC/EFTA join to become largest free-trade area
British-Spanish agreement on Gibraltar

Uganda suspends military ties with US
Talks on Namibian settlement
Sudan declares state of emergency
Military coup in Guinea/Conte president
South Africa/Mozambique nonaggression treaty
France and Libya withdraw from Chad
Reagan criticizes South African apartheid

US/Iraq restore full diplomatic relations
Jordan/Egypt political ties restored
Morocco/Libya treaty establishes "Union of States"
U.N. resolution calls for Israeli withdrawal from Lebanon
France sells arms to Saudi Arabia
Fatah and 4 other PLO factions unite
Egypt/USSR resume diplomatic relations
U.N. reports Iraqi use of chemical weapons against Iran
Egypt rejoins Islamic Conference Organization
China/USSR increase trade
Clashes in Jammu and Kashmir
Demonstrations against Marcos in Manila
Indira Gandhi assassinated/Son Rajiv prime minister

Violence in Sri Lanka

Uruguay paralyzed by general strike
Nicaragua charges US abuses in World Court
Castro calls for improved US-Cuban relations

1985

Chernenko dies
Gorbachev chosen head of CPSU
Reagan commits U.S. to Strategic Defense Initiative (SDI) program
Geneva Summit Reagan/Gorbachev
USSR unilateral moratorium on nuclear testing
USSR allows International Atomic Energy Agency (IAEA) to conduct nuclear
inspections

Spain joins COCOM
Anglo-Irish accord on Northern Ireland
Spain and Portugal enter EC
Jaruzelski resigns
Greenland resigns from EC

Lebanese Shiites hijack TWA flight from Athens-Rome
Terry Anderson kidnapped in Beirut
Israeli troops withdraw from Lebanon
Israeli jets bomb PLO headquarters in Tunis
PLO moves headquarters from Tunis to Baghdad
Libya/Iran sign Strategic Alliance Treaty
Italian oceanliner *Achille Lauro* hijacked by Palestinians
Jordan/Syria open diplomatic relations
Egyptian airliner hijacked
King Hussein joins Mubarak peace effort in Middle East

U.N. condemns South Africa for killing protestors
Food riots in Sudan
U.S. sanctions against South Africa
Tunisia/Libya cut diplomatic relations
Doe wins Liberian presidential election
Sudan/Libya establish diplomatic relations and military protocol
South Africa withdraws from southern Angola

Indonesia/China sign trade agreement
France/China 5-year trade agreement
Sino-British declaration on Hong Kong ratified
Greenpeace ship *Rainbow Warrior* sunk off coast of New Zealand
U.S. lifts 1/2 COCOM technology restrictions to China
Indonesia/USSR trade protocol
7 Asian countries establish SAARC
North Korea signs Nuclear Non-Proliferation Treaty
China agrees to IAEA nuclear inspections

US imposes economic sanctions on Nicaragua
US Congress approves aid to Contras
Mexico City hit by earthquakes
EC signs 5-year cooperative agreement with 6 Central American nations

---

1986

Space shuttle *Challenger* explodes
Reagan/Mulroney sign 5-year extension of NORAD
Reagan/Gorbachev Reykjavik Summit
Congress signs Anti-Apartheid Act

Spain and Portugal join EC
Spain/Israel establish diplomatic ties
Mitterrand/Thatcher announce plans for English Channel tunnel
Bomb explodes in West Berlin discotheque
Bomb explodes TWA jet enroute from Rome-Athens
Nazi victim Elie Wiesel wins Nobel Peace Prize
EC Accord on Counterterrorism
US and EC announce sanctions against Syria

Gorbachev announces Soviet economic reforms
Chernobyl explosion
Poland admitted to International Monetary Fund (IMF)
Gorbachev proposes ban on nuclear weapons by year 2000
Swedish prime minister Olaf Palme dead
Dubinin appointed new Soviet ambassador to US
US/USSR education and science exchanges announced

Civil war in South Yemen
Egyptian/Israeli summit (Mubarak/Peres)
Peres resigns/Shamir forms new government
Home rule reestablished in Kashmir and Jammu
Najibullah replaces Karmal as general-secretary of Afghanistan
Soviets announce partial withdrawal from Afghanistan
Martial law ended in Bangladesh

China submits application to join GATT
China announces "Three Obstacles" to Sino-Soviet talks
Chinese students demonstrate in Shanghai/Beijing
South Korea pushes for constitutional reform/Riots result
Marcos deposed

State of emergency in South Africa
U.N. General Assembly special session on African economic crisis
Nigeria/Britain restore full diplomatic ties
Pass laws abolished in South Africa

Duvalier ousted in Haiti
Mexico admitted to GATT
San Salvador earthquake

1987

Glasnost, perestroika introduced
INF treaty signed
First successful launching of Titan 3-B rocket
US/Canada/Japan/European space agencies announce cooperation on space
station
Protesters march against U.S. policy in Central America
U.S./Canada Trade Pact
Canadian "Meech Lake" agreement
Arias wins Nobel Peace Prize

Creation of joint French/West German army brigade
Trial of Nazi Klaus Barbie
Gorbachev accuses party of stagnation/failures
Yeltsin dismissed as Moscow party chief

Strikes in Yugoslavia
West German Mathias Rust flies into Red Square
State of emergency in Romania
Pope visits Walesa/Poland
Soviets deploy mobile SS-24 ICBMs

State Department bars US citizens' travel to Lebanon
US/Soviets offer protection to Kuwaiti oil tankers in Persian Gulf
Egypt breaks diplomatic ties with Iran
US frigate *Stark* struck by 2 Iraqi missiles in Persian Gulf
U.N. Security Council calls for Iran-Iraq cease-fire (Resolution 598)
Sri Lankan Parliament grants limited autonomy to Tamil majority
Pakistani nuclear capability acknowledged
India imposes direct rule on Punjab state/sends police to counter violence

U.S. and Mongolia establish diplomatic relations
Toshiba accused of selling sensitive submarine technology to USSR
New South Korean constitution and elections
Marshall Islands and Federated States of Micronesia released from US/U.N.
trusteeship
Attempted coup in Manila

Students demonstrate in Beijing
China and Portugal sign agreement to return Macao to the PRC in 1999
Conservative Chinese leaders forced to retire from Central Committee
during 13th Communist Party Congress

Haitians approve new constitution
Arias Regional Peace Plan signed by five Central American nations
Group of Eight Latin American nations meets in Acapulco
Earthquakes in Ecuador
Brazil and Argentina sign accords providing for common currency
Peru nationalizes private banks

South Africa and Mozambique renew Joint Security Commission
U.N. Security Council condemns South Africa actions in Angola/demands
withdrawal

1988

START negotiations stop
Agreement reached on Angola, Namibia

Bhutto elected
Afghanistan war ended/Geneva Accords signed

U.N. peacekeepers win Nobel Prize
Summer Olympic games held in Seoul

PLO recognizes Israel, declares independent statehood, and opens dialogue with
US
US/Iranian naval forces clash in Gulf

Estonia asserts right to veto Soviet laws
Supreme Soviet creates new governmental system
Gorbachev announces unilateral force cuts

1989

Iran-Contra scandal
Bush becomes U.S. president
San Francisco earthquake
World Bank and IMF endorse Brady Plan

Botha resigns; DeKlerk elected
Angolan civil war talks open

Thousands killed in Tiananmen Square
Independence demonstrations shock Tibet
Vietnamese announce exit from Cambodia

Stroessner ousted in Paraguay
Venezuelans riot over rising prices
Noriega voids election

Solidarity legalized

Ethnic violence erupts in Yugoslavia
Hungary dismantles border fence
Honecker resigns
Kohl-Gorbachev declare right of states to choose political system
Berlin Wall comes down
Ceausescu executed in Romania
Havel elected president of Czechoslovakia

Syria-Iran sign Lebanon Peace Pact

Soviet withdrawal from Afghanistan begins
First Soviet nationwide multi-candidate election held; Yeltsin wins in Russia
Troops gas demonstrators in Tbilisi, Georgia
START restarts
Gorbachev elected president of USSR
Ethnic clashes in Uzbekistan
Half a million miners strike in USSR
Lithuanian party votes to break with Moscow

1990

President de Klerk legalizes African National Congress (ANC) in South Africa
Mandela released from prison
Namibia gains independence
Mobutu ends one-party rule
Ivory Coast legalizes opposition
Tambo returns to the ANC
Kaunda legalizes opposition

Aquino calls for reconciliation in Philippines
Prodemocracy demonstrations in Nepal
Kashmiri violence escalates
Bhutto dismissed for corruption
Students riot and demand Ershad resignation in Bangladesh
Ershad resigns
Ethnic violence breaks out in Hyderabad

Martial law lifted in Beijing
Prodemocracy protests held in Ulan Bator
Martial law lifted for Tibet

President Lee calls for ending war state in Taiwan

Chamorro defeats Ortega in Nicaragua
Contra leaders agree to break camps
US invades Panama
Noriega deposed and arrested
US-Mexican free trade talks proposed
Menem gives military new internal powers
Trujillo elected in Colombia
President Fujimori takes office in Peru

Prodemocracy demonstrations rock Kuwait
Kuwaiti opposition boycotts elections
Yemen created
Iraq invades Kuwait
Palestinians riot at Temple Mount
UN authorizes force against Iraq

Germany unified
CEMA adopts free trade principles
Bulgarian Communist party loses power guarantee
Czech Communist party loses 100 seats
Soviet-Czech agreement on troop withdrawal reached
Ethnic clashes in Romania
First Hungarian parliamentary elections held
Bulgaria approves multi-candidate elections
Hungarian Parliament authorizes withdrawal from Warsaw Pact
Dubcek elected parliamentary chair
Prodemocracy demonstrations in Albania
Walesa runs for presidency

Ethnic violence in Baku
Riots in Tadzhikistan
Prodemocracy marches in 32 Soviet cities
Georgian Parliament denounces 1921 annexation
Lithuania declares independence
Estonian Parliament declares transition to independence
Latvia declares independence from Soviet Union
Yeltsin elected Russian president
Armenian Republic declares independence
Russian Parliament declares control over resources
Gorbachev asks for emergency powers
Shevardnadze resigns

Recommended Readings

Bienen, Henry S., and Nicolas van de Walle. *Of Time and Power: Leadership Duration in the Modern World* (Stanford, Calif.: Stanford University Press, 1991).

Billington, James H. *Russia Transformed: Breakthrough to Hope* (New York: The Free Press, 1992).

Brandon, Henry, ed. *In Search of a New World Order: The Future of U.S.- European Relations* (Washington, D.C.: The Brookings Institution, 1992).

Brown, Lester R. *State of the World 1992* (New York: W.W. Norton & Company, 1992).

Brown, Seyom. *International Relations in a Changing Global System: Toward a Theory of the World Polity* (Boulder, Colo.: Westview Press, 1992).

Brown, Sheryl J., and Kimber M. Schraub, eds. *Resolving Third World Conflict: Challenges for a New Era* (Washington, D.C.: United States Institute of Peace Press, 1992).

Brzezinski, Zbigniew. "Post-Victory Blues" (Washington, D.C.: Georgetown University, School of Foreign Service, Academy of World Inquiry, 1990).

Carnegie Endowment National Commission Report. *Changing Our Ways: America and the New World* (Washington, D.C.: Carnegie Endowment for International Peace, 1992).

Crocker, Chester A. "Peace-Making and Military Power" (Washington, D.C.: Georgetown University, School of Foreign Service, Academy of World Inquiry, 1991).

Davidson, Jonathan, ed. *The European Community in the Nineties* (Washington, D.C.: EC Delegation to the United States, 1992).

de Blij, Harm J., and Peter O. Muller. *Physical Geography of the Global Environment* (New York: John Wiley & Sons, 1993).

Dunn, Lewis A. *Containing Nuclear Proliferation.* Adelphi Papers 263 (Oxford: Brassey's, 1991).

Feinberg, Richard E., and Delia M. Boylan. *Modular Multilateralism: North-South Economic Relations in the 1990's* (Washington, D.C.: Overseas Development Council, 1991).

Frederick, Howard H. *Global Communication and International Relations* (Belmont, Calif.: Wadsworth Publishing Company, 1992).

Freedom House Survey Team. *Freedom in the World: Political Rights and Civil Liberties, 1991-1992* (New York: Freedom House, 1992).

Fukuyama, Francis. *The End of History and the Last Man* (New York: Maxwell Macmillan International, 1992).

Gore, Albert. *Earth in the Balance: Ecology and the Human Spirit* (Boston: Houghton Mifflin, 1992).

Haftendorn, Helga, and Christian Tuschhoff, eds. *America and Europe in an Era of Change* (Boulder, Colo.: Westview Press, 1993).

Halberstam, David. *The Next Century* (New York: Morrow, 1991).

Hardison, O.B. *Disappearing Through the Skylight: Culture and Technology in the Twentieth Century* (New York: Viking Press, 1989).

Hawking, Stephen. *A Brief History of Time: From the Big Bang to Black Holes* (New York: Bantam Books, 1988).

Henderson, Hazel. *Paradigms in Progress: Life Beyond Economics* (Indianapolis, Ind.: Knowledge Systems Inc., 1991).

Huntington, Samuel. *The Third Wave: Democratization in the Late Twentieth Century* (Norman, Okla.: University of Oklahoma Press, 1991).

Institute for the Study of Diplomacy Report. *The Foreign Service in 2001* (Washington, D.C.: Institute for the Study of Diplomacy, Georgetown University, School of Foreign Service, 1992).

Johnson, Paul. *The Birth of the Modern: World Society 1815-1830* (New York: HarperCollins, 1991).

———. *Modern Times: The World from the Twenties to the Nineties* (New York: HarperCollins, 1991).

Keen, Peter G.W. *Shaping the Future: Business Design Through Information Technology* (Boston: Harvard Business School Press, 1991).

Kegley, Charles W., Jr., ed. *The Long Postwar Peace: Contending Explanations and Projections* (New York: HarperCollins, 1991).

Kennedy, Paul. *The Rise and Fall of the Great Powers: Economic Change and Military Conflict from 1500 to 2000* (New York: Random House, 1987).

Lambeth, Benjamin S. *Desert Storm and Its Meaning: The View from Moscow* (Santa Monica, Calif.: RAND, 1992).

Lightman, Alan. *Ancient Light: Our Changing View of the Universe* (Cambridge: Harvard University Press, 1991).

Lynn-Jones, Sean M., and Steven E. Miller. *America's Strategy in a Changing World* (Cambridge: The MIT Press, 1992).

Maier, Charles S. *Why Did Communism Collapse in 1989?* Program on Central and Eastern Europe Working Paper Series (Cambridge: Harvard University, 1991).

Mathews, Jessica Tuchman, ed. *Preserving the Global Environment: The Challenge of Shared Leadership* (New York: W.W. Norton & Company, 1991).

McGhee, George C. *International Community: A Goal for a New World Order* (Lanham, Md.: University Press of America, 1992).

Mokyr, Joel. *The Lever of Riches: Technological Creativity and Economic Progress* (New York: Oxford University Press, 1990).

Morison, Elting E. *Men, Machines, and Modern Times* (Cambridge: MIT Press, 1989).

Mortimer, Edward. *Adelphi Papers* "European Security After the Cold War" (Oxford: Brassey's, 1992).

Muravchik, Joshua. *Exporting Democracy: Fulfilling America's Destiny* (Lanham, Md.: American Enterprise Institute, 1992).

Nye, Joseph S., Jr., Kurt Biedenkopf, and Motoo Shiina. *Global Cooperation After the Cold War: A Reassessment of Trilateralism* (New York: The Trilateral Commission, 1991).

Oye, Kenneth A., Robert J. Lieber, and Donald Rothchild. *Eagle in a New World: American Grand Strategy in the Post-Cold War Era* (New York: HarperCollins, 1992).

Revel, Jean-Francois. *How Democracies Perish* (Garden City, New York: Doubleday & Company, 1983).

Rizopoulos, Nicholas X., ed. *Sea-Changes: American Foreign Policy in a World Transformed* (New York: Council on Foreign Relations Press, 1990).

Rosenau, James N. *Global Voices: Dialogues in International Relations* (Boulder, Colo.: Westview Press, 1993).

Taylor, Charles. *Multiculturalism and "The Politics of Recognition"* (Princeton, N.J.: Princeton University Press, 1992).

The United States, Europe and the Structures of a New World Order. Proceedings of an International Conference held at Georgetown University on October 17 and 18, 1991 (Munich: Herbert Quandt Foundation, 1992).

Treverton, Gregory F. *America, Germany, and the Future of Europe* (Princeton, N.J.: Princeton University Press, A Council on Foreign Relations Book, 1992).

Williams, Abiodun, ed. *Many Voices: Multilateral Negotiations in the World Arena* (Boulder, Colo.: Westview Press, 1992).

Woo-Cumings, Meredith, and Michael Loriaux, eds. *Past as Prelude: History in the Making of a New World Order* (Boulder, Colo.: Westview Press, 1993).

Working Group on U.S. Diplomacy Toward the Commonwealth of Independent States (Washington, D.C.: Institute for the Study of Diplomacy, Georgetown University, School of Foreign Service, 1992).

Wriston, Walter. *The Twilight of Sovereignty: How the Information Revolution Is Transforming our World* (New York: Scribners, 1992).

About the Book and Author

We may not be able to predict the future with accuracy, but only at our peril do we ignore imaginative forecasts. Allan Goodman charts the future as historians map the past and in the process uncovers trends that counter conventional wisdom about persistent world problems such as ethnic conflict, environmental degradation, and economic injustice.

Just as very few anticipated the fall of the Berlin Wall and the vast changes that followed, many will resist Goodman's vision of a society in which people and robots work side by side and an international polity focuses on the principles of cooperation, interdependency, multilateralism, and interculturalism rather than on conflict models of the nation-state.

Looking at the interaction of four central tendencies—democratization, technological expansion, regional integration, and the obsolescence of war—the author sketches a picture of a future imbued with ideas, populated by "ordinary heroes," and governed by the power of vision. Throughout, Goodman's own extraordinary vision is highlighted in breaks from the text to featured previews of news headlines for the 1990s, a series of special information boxes, and a provocative list of 100 inventions/discoveries for the twenty-first century.

Challenging and engaging for specialists, students, and general readers alike, *A Brief History of the Future* is sure to spark the investigation, indignation, and (the author hopes most of all) imagination that the future requires.

Allan E. Goodman is associate dean of the School of Foreign Service at Georgetown University. He has held a variety of positions in and out of government; he is a consultant to policymakers, journalists, and others; and he has authored or edited numerous books and articles, including *The Lost Peace: America's Search for a Negotiated Settlement of the Vietnam War* and *Strategic Intelligence and American National Security* (with Bruce D. Berkowitz).

Index